FERMANAGH
ITS SPECIAL LANDSCAPES
A Study of the Fermanagh Countryside
and Its Heritage

BELFAST : HMSO

Foreword by Caldwell Mc Claughry   *Foreword by Richard Needham*

I welcome the publication of the work that has been undertaken by the Department of the Environment, Countryside and Wildlife Branch on the landscapes of Fermanagh. I believe that many people appreciate the beauty and richness of the County's natural assets and it is right that every effort should be made to inform so that we can be fully aware in all our decision making for the future.

It is also vital that in any policy related to conservation, we should always give rightful consideration to the need for development, especially for people who live and wish to remain living in the countryside and who should be encouraged with a confident outlook for the future of our rural areas.

This work that is now presented is an important contribution to that confidence for the people of County Fermanagh and I wish to thank those directly involved for the work that has been undertaken, especially with a commitment to a better quality of life for our people

Caldwell McClaughry
Chairman, Fermanagh District Council.

Fermanagh is renowned for its tranquil beauty, unique wildlife and diverse heritage. Over the years a strong farming and business community has shaped a place of special identity with confidence and continuity of purpose.

Fermanagh must, however, change to meet the aspirations of the people and satisfy the needs of a more demanding population. It has always been a place of great interest and enjoyment, and I have been happy to see the tremendous enthusiasm of the people and the District Council in building on their environmental assets for their economic well-being and to the delight of those who visit there. They realise the importance of getting the balance right not only for themselves but for the future generations who will live in or tour the area. It is important, therefore, that there should be a free and open discussion about this matter.

My Department has prepared this document not only for the enjoyment of many but also as a contribution to this discussion. The direction of change and its environmental impacts can be influenced by many Departments, Agencies and people. The document provides background information for all of us to consider the role of conservation in the future of Fermanagh.

Richard Needham MP
Parliamentary Under-Secretary of State

ACKNOWLEDGEMENTS

This report has been in preparation over a period of two years and many people have contributed. The Department acknowledges the hard work of staff of the Countryside and Wildlife Branch and their consultant, Joyce McCormick. Special thanks are owed to all those people who have commented on the draft text.

Unless otherwise accredited, photographs in the text are the property of the Department's Countryside and Wildlife and Historic Monuments and Buildings Branches; particular thanks to Robert Thompson, Gail Pollock and Andrew Stott. Thanks also to the Northern Ireland Tourist Board, Ron Thompson and Raymond Humphreys, Impartial Reporter.

Quotations in the text have been reproduced with the kind permission of The Institute of Irish Studies, The Queen's University of Belfast; The Blackstaff Press, Dundonald; The Friar's Bush Press, Belfast; The O'Brien Press Ltd, Dublin; Dr James Cruickshank; The Royal Irish Academy, Dublin, and the Governors and Guardians of Armagh Public Library (from the original held in the Library).

Maps and diagrams are reproduced with kind permission of the Ordnance Survey for Northern Ireland and the Department of Environmental Studies, University of Ulster. Many thanks also to Alastair Laverty for cartography.

CONTENTS

S U M M A R Y

PART A FERMANAGH'S RURAL SCENE

1 FERMANAGH IN CONTEXT

Fermanagh is located peripherally in the British Isles and Europe. Landscapes and heritage reflect this location. Fermanagh remains an undiscovered land of quiet waters and misty hills, a place where wildlife survives in rare habitats and where old customs die hard.

2 LOWLAND, LAKES AND MOUNTAINS

In the Erne basin, land and water co-exist in a multitude of scales and interlocking ways which give beauty and variety to visual impressions. Lowlands with confused hills and loughs are in marked contrast with rugged uplands and limestone escarpments.

3 THE HERITAGE OF DAYS GONE BY

Fermanagh has a unique blend of Prehistoric, Early Christian, Medieval and Plantation period monuments well-preserved in the countryside. In later history, estates, towns, farms, roads and industry profoundly affected today's landscape.

4 A RICH WILDLIFE

Fermanagh is internationally renowned for the abundance and variety of its wildlife. Important habitats include mountain and moorland, limestone grasslands, woodland, lowland bog, wetland and loughs. A number of increasingly rare species of plants, birds and insects survive in these areas.

5 THE COUNTRYSIDE AND USE OF THE LAND

Farmers, and other workers of the land, have made the Fermanagh countryside. Traditional farm practices are reflected in the landscape - fields, hedges, hay-meadows, turf banks, lanes, farmhouses and sheds. Agriculture remains dominant in the rural economy.

6 CONSERVATION AND RURAL DEVELOPMENT

Conservation aims to protect the environmental assets of the countryside, to enhance its qualities wherever possible and to ensure the wise and sustainable use of its resources. Conservation does not necessarily oppose development but instead it tries to ensure that development leads to an improved environment and long-term benefits to the community. Fermanagh has some very special qualities and future conservation raises a number of important issues - an agenda for conservation includes issues which affect landscapes, farming, wildlife, woodland and forestry, heritage, housing and development, mineral workings, recreation and tourism.

PART B SPECIAL LANDSCAPES

Sixteen distinct landscapes are defined and briefly described. Their special qualities are assessed and some of the particular conservation issues are identified. The Special Landscapes are:

1 The Erne Lakeland

2 The Sillees Valley

3 The Knockmore Scarpland

4 The Lough Navar and Ballintempo Uplands

5 The Garrison Lowlands

6 The Lough Macnean Valley

7 Cuilcagh and Marlbank

8 The Arney Lowlands

9 Slieve Russel, Derrylin and Kinawley

10 Newtownbutler and Rosslea Lowlands

11 Carnrock and Cooneen Hills

12 Colebrooke and Tempo River Valley

13 Topped and Brougher Mountain Uplands

14 Ballinamallard and Irvinestown Lowlands

15 Glendarragh and Bannagh River Valleys

16 Croagh and Garvary River

Part A
FERMANAGH'S RURAL SCENE

....The face of this country is infinitely variegated,

and affords in summer to a person standing on one

of its mountains Bennaughlin, Colcogh or

Bellmore, one of the most curious and entertaining

prospects in Europe. Vast mountains descending

into large valleys beautified with lawns, lakes,

rivers and infinite numbers of small rising hills,

which are covered with corn, herds or flocks, and

generally skirted with small wood and a little

brook twisting round. In the midst Lough Erne

flowing like a sea interspersed with 400 islands of

all sorts of sizes and figures with gentlemen's seats

and towns. From this vast basin the land rising

again on each side by degrees, first in flat

meadows green as beds of leeks, extended along

its shores, then in small hills, variegated with corn

and cattle, and terminating in mountains which

seem to touch the clouds....

> *William Henry, 1739* [1]

Drumgay Lough

Northern Ireland has within its small area a remarkably wide diversity of landscapes which range from the high granite peaks of the Mountains of Mourne to the deeply cut Glens of Antrim, and from the great sea loughs like Strangford with its multitude of islands to the geometric regularity of the famous Giant's Causeway. The Fermanagh lakes and their surrounding hills and limestone caves are an important and distinctive part of this diversity.

Fermanagh, the south-west corner of Northern Ireland, is located on the periphery of the British Isles and Europe, some 400 miles (650 kilometres) from London and 700 miles (1100 kilometres) from Paris. This fringe position, both in a physical and cultural sense, has

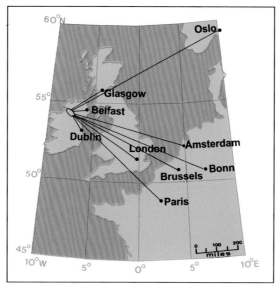

Fermanagh in Europe

contributed much to its distinctive landscapes and heritage. In prehistory and throughout history people were able to navigate around the western seaways of Europe and those who entered Fermanagh left behind their particular legacy. Today such a peripheral location has some economic disadvantages, including for example expensive communications with the rest of the United Kingdom and the continental European Community, but it has helped the county retain much of its traditional character, a valuable asset for the growing tourist industry.

The landscapes of Fermanagh are a blend of land and freshwater in a variety of scales and form. There are large expanses of lough water, lesser bays broken by a maze of islands, and away from the major loughs, a network of water channels and rivers winding their often indirect routes through lowlands tightly packed with drumlin hills. All this is set against a background of rugged hills and crags which rise abruptly from the lowlands below.

The prevailing westerly winds bring moist air, from the Atlantic, noted for its freshness and freedom from industrial pollutants. Temperatures are never extreme and grasses and woodland grow luxuriantly along with many lichens, mosses and aquatic plants. The abundant freshwater in loughs, rivers and mountain streams, supports large numbers of coarse and game fish and the water, woods, bogs and meadows are the habitats for many birds, a refuge from development and pollution elsewhere in Europe. Whilst favourable for wildlife, the heavy Fermanagh soils and moist climate have always been a constraint for farmers, but in working around the difficulties traditional farm practices evolved which were sensitive to nature and the landscape.

The area is steeped in history and tradition with many remnants of prehistory and history assembled together in a complexity as yet only partly understood. Ancient stone monuments, settlements of early farmers, island monasteries, ruined medieval churches and Plantation castles and, still in use, churches and great houses of more recent times; all co-exist in an atmosphere of reverence for the past.

Enniskillen, the county town, and other small towns and villages are located throughout the area, but much of the population lives in the countryside and it is in the rural townlands that many traditional ways of life continue. The pace of life is relatively slow and kinship ties are strong. The people are charming and witty, sometimes

Thatched house, Derrycanon

mischievous but kindly to man and beast. In their homes and through their lifestyle can be seen the strong combination of cultural heritage and the adaptation to

the local environment. It is these people who face the challenge of looking after the countryside for the future.

In the Europe of the 1990s Fermanagh remains an undiscovered land of quiet waters and misty hills, a place where wildlife survives in rare habitats, where old customs die hard and where the landscape reflects a

long-established relationship between people and nature. Change and development are inevitable, and indeed in some respects highly desirable, but their effects on the special character of Fermanagh need not be destructive.

Lower Lough Erne

Derrycanon Lough

Jokingly it is said "half of the year Lough Erne is in Fermanagh while in the other half Fermanagh is in Lough Erne" - and because of the frequency of winter floods this may have an element of truth. What is for certain, however, is that in the Erne basin, land and water co-exist in a multitude of scales and inter-locking ways which give variety to visual impressions yet make it difficult to perceive any overall picture.

In the closed-in, small-world intimacy of the infinite valleys, hollows, hills and lake basins of the lowlands, tight-packed tall hedgerows block the views and houses hide around corners in clumps of trees. Vistas open suddenly from bends in the road giving a glimpse of silvery waters, richly coloured reed beds and a flock of

geese or swans. Cattle graze the ubiquitous rolling fields of grass differentiated by the haze of wild flowers, the spikes of rushes and the bright greens of fertilized ryegrass. The surrounding hills seem to lurk on the horizon, rarely out of sight but always an immeasurable distance away, picked out by their distinctive profiles. The true drama of these hills and their sometimes precipitous edges is only appreciated at close range.

In sharp contrast are the panoramas afforded by hilltop or lough-shore viewpoints, where the land is laid out as a sea of rippling drumlins lapping against the large bulk of the surrounding hills and partly submerged beneath a

Knockmore and Sillees Valley

sheet of water. Rivers merge with channels and loughs, and drumlin hills run into promontories and beads of islands. At this scale individual fields are lost in a cloak of trees and houses appear as white speckles.

Escarpments at Knockmore

Fermanagh's broad landscape of lowland, lakes and hills is largely a left-over from the last Ice Age when glaciers scoured out great basins in the underlying sandstone, shale and limestone rocks. As the glaciers melted, the lowlands were covered in a thick layer of boulder clay moulded into countless drumlin hills, hollows and ridges. The over-deepened basins quickly flooded with water and overflowing streams linked up to form the complex River Erne waterway.

The uplands avoided much of the boulder clay cover and their ice-sharpened escarpments of limestone and sandstone remain dramatic topographical features. However, as if unhappy with their naked state, nature contrived to cloak the bare upland plateau in blanket bog which has built up over the last few thousand years.

Cuilcagh Mountain

Only the rims of limestone rocks, which form magnificent outcrops at Knockmore, Benaughlin and Hanging Rock, were sufficiently well drained to prevent peat formation. These limestones are riddled with underground rivers and their caves are amongst the most spectacular in Ireland.

At the core of Fermanagh is the Lough Erne basin, cutting through the county as a diagonal from south-east to north-west. Two major water bodies, the Upper and Lower Loughs, lie within the basin, joined by a network of water channels and minor loughs, all part of the River Erne itself. Both the source of the river and its outlet to the sea are situated in the Republic of Ireland, thus Fermanagh's waterway should be considered in its wider regional context.

Lower Lough Erne

The Erne lakes are generally edged by lowland, but moving away from the lakes in any direction one rapidly becomes aware of a change in landscape, particular to specific areas but, most obviously, a marked contrast between west and east Fermanagh.

To the south and west of the loughs the lowlands are bounded by a high range of hills culminating in the flat-topped ridge of Cuilcagh Mountain. The hills are broken into blocks by the wide valleys of the Arney River extending to the west, and the Cladagh or Swanlinbar River extending to the south. Folded and faulted strata of limestone, sandstone and shales run through the hills causing sharp breaks in topography, rocky outcrops, escarpments and broken plateaus. To the west, towards Garrison and Lough Melvin, the upland plateau slips gradually back down towards sea-level forming an open lowland exposed directly to Atlantic weather sweeping inland across Donegal Bay. The Arney valley narrows to the west and Lough Macnean, broken into two parts by a land bridge at

Belcoo, is a much more sheltered and enclosed lough basin than Lough Erne. Soils in west Fermanagh are generally poor for agricultural purposes.

To the north and east of the loughs the lowland areas are more extensive and the hills less dramatic. Drumlin hills emerge at the lough shore to spread in all directions, filling the broad valleys between the lines of higher hills which rise to Slieve Beagh, Brougher Mountain and Tappaghan Mountain on the county boundary with Tyrone. The size, shape and orientation of the hills varies from place to place and, although never dominant in the landscape, the river corridors of the Kesh/Glendarragh, Ballinamallard, Tempo, Colebrooke and Finn-Lacky Rivers add a thread of continuity through a seemingly chaotic landscape. The uplands are diverse but in contrast to those of west Fermanagh the slopes are smoother and the hilltops rounded. Deep valleys and glens penetrate and break open the hills, sheltering isolated farming communities.

Drumlin countryside near Lack

FERMANAGH DISTRICT

Source : University of Ulster

Cairn on Topped Mountain

Fermanagh's archaeology provides a record of cultural change through time, of how different societies adapted to and modified the difficult physical environment. Its perimeter of mountains, its hills, lakes, lowland bogs and forests were hard to cross, routes were easy to defend and within Fermanagh one could simply get lost in thickly-wooded lowland. However, whilst the land was divided by so much water, the loughs and rivers provided a through route connecting to the western seaboard at Ballyshannon and via the short overland routes to the Shannon system in the interior of Ireland.

There is some evidence that the earliest settlers in Fermanagh date back to the Mesolithic period, over 8,000 years ago. These people lived by hunting, fishing and collecting berries along the lough shores. Then, some 6,000 years ago, the first farmers arrived and sought out the lighter limestone or sandier/gravelly soils where the land could be more easily cultivated. On the favoured hill slopes great stone burial monuments - court, portal, passage and wedge tombs - record the slowly changing fashions and beliefs of these early farming communities.

About 4,000 years ago a new, metalworking technology reached Fermanagh. Whilst continuing the woodland clearance and pastoral way of life, the Bronze Age people displayed more individualistic traits and placed human remains in small stone cists or individual graves, some in round hilltop cairns such as on Knockninny and Topped Mountain. Other impressive landscape features of the Bronze Age are round barrows, standing stones and stone circles, but perhaps most interesting of all is the distinctive rock art, not found with such frequency elsewhere in Ulster and sharing similarities with work in Spain.

There followed a shadowy period of prehistory, the Iron Age, which brought newcomers who could tackle the heavier forest soils for the first time. These newcomers, Celtic speaking peoples, were small conquering groups who imposed their language and technology on the Irish before them. Surviving from this period are some unusual and impressive stone heads and figures which are thought to be manifestations of pagan religious beliefs. In an ancient graveyard on Boa Island the two faced Janus figure with large, somewhat menacing eyes, is quite remarkable.

Cup and Ring Marked Stone, Reyfad

Stone Alignment at Montiaghroe
Janus Figure, Boa Island

Rath at Lisblake

and perhaps livestock and they were often sited at vantage points in the better-drained lower hill and drumlin country. About 600 ring-forts survive today and the rings feature in a rich folk tradition. They are often recognised as the dwellings of fairies, as places of mystical music, supernatural lights and noises, and stories abound on the penalties suffered for interfering with these sites or the thorn bushes growing upon them.

Surviving raths are situated mainly on hilltops or hillside spurs and often, with a thick growth of trees, they provide prominent landscape features. In the 18th and 19th centuries, it was fashionable on large estates to reinforce this image by planting raths with trees and, in places, creating tree-rings in imitation of ancient forts.

The Early Christian period which began in the 5th century AD contributed much to the heritage of Fermanagh. The most widespread monuments of this period are circular farmsteads enclosed either by one or more rings of earthen bank and ditch (raths) or a drystone wall (cashels). These enclosures, known as 'forts', presumably had a defensive purpose for people

Another defensive settlement form of the Early Christian period which continued in use up to the 17th century was the crannog or artificial island. Crannogs were generally built in small loughs separated from the main Lough Erne waterway. They have survived as small, densely wooded islands - sometimes even two, three or four in one lough. Excavations have revealed finds of pottery, querns and other everyday items.

Many present-day 'townlands' may have their origin in early farms. Ancient settlement place-name elements in Old Irish *dun, rath, lios, cathair* and *caiseal* can be traced in some townland names, for example, Procklis, Lissagorry Glebe, Lislea and Rathkeelan, while the townland boundaries almost certainly maintain age-old territorial divisions. These boundaries generally follow physical features, such as rivers or crest lines and lake centres, all of significance in landscape terms, but it is their particular local identity which is most important to rural dwellers. Individual townlands have their locally well-known characteristics such as soil quality, topography, farm structure and history, and it is to townlands that country people, especially farmers, feel they belong. Thus townlands and their names are elements of heritage for which there is special pride and concern.

Crannog, Drumgay Lough

Side by side with the raths, cashels and crannogs of the Early Christian period was a range of ecclesiastical settlements. The Erne formed a great waterway, and many early churches are on its islands and shores: not isolated retreats but on Fermanagh's watery 'main road' They served the scattered rural population, maintained the round of worship, and offered hospitality for travellers and education for scholars.

Monasteries, founded on Devenish, Cleenish, Inishmacsaint and other islands, continued in use through the Medieval period. Devenish was a large community and a centre of scholarship, but other churches were smaller, serving a family or a local area. From the 9th and 10th centuries there are carved stone crosses at Boho, Lisnaskea and Galloon, and the famous carved figures on White Island and at Killadeas are of similar date. The churches of Lough Erne suffered from Viking raids and nothing is left above

Statue, White Island

Devenish

ground of their early buildings, built of wood. The earliest stone buildings date from the 12th century: the little church known as St Molaise's House and the fine round tower on Devenish and the door on White Island. From later centuries there is an important group of ruined medieval parish churches, many of them on the same sites as the Early Christian churches. During the Middle Ages the Erne served as the main pilgrim route to St Patrick's Purgatory in Lough Derg, and some of Fermanagh's churches offered 'guest-house' accommodation to travellers from as far away as France and Italy.

Whilst the church established its presence on the islands and shores and clearance of farmland continued, local leaders, using water channels for travel and hilltops for defence, gradually established a largely independent 'kingdom', Fermanagh.

In fact, in the 1,000 years up to the 17th century, Fermanagh was almost untouched by the mainstream of European history: the waves of colonisation, subjugation and war experienced elsewhere in Great Britain and Ireland did not reach the highly impenetrable north-west of Ireland. The passing of pilgrims and scholars no doubt brought news of these events from the outside world but, until the end of the 16th century, Fermanagh was under the control of the Maguires, one of the powerful Gaelic clans of Ulster.

Many of the archaeological sites have survived because they have always been regarded with respect or superstition by local people. But whilst there are obvious remains of some chambered graves and raths, most associated older farms and fields have long since disappeared beneath successive farm improvements. Only where the spread of blanket bog has hidden and protected some minor features, or on hillsides which escaped later improvements, is it possible to find a more complete picture of the ancient landscape. Lake muds and lowland mires have also helped our understanding of the past by preserving canoes, and cots, the predecessors of the present-day flat bottomed boats still in use in a few places in the Erne waterway.

At the beginning of the 17th century some long threads with the past were broken and a succession of events led to profound changes which introduced new elements to the heritage and landscapes of Fermanagh. The changes also had major effects on population, community life and livelihood.

By 1600 no fixed villages or towns existed in Fermanagh but the castles at Enniskillen and Lisnaskea, both held by Maguire chiefs, may have been the centres

Tully Castle

of administration. Then, in 1607, when James I gained control of west Ulster, the Gaelic chiefs took 'flight' and from 1610 English and Scottish planters and settlers began to arrive in Fermanagh.

The planters, having been granted land, established a series of large estates, many originally with castles or fortified farmhouses, around the lough shores and astride the main lines of land communications: Castle Archdale, Castlecaldwell, Crom, Florence Court, Colebrooke, Castle Balfour, Necarne, Castle Coole, Castle Hume and Spring Grove. Many original estate castles and bawns have been rebuilt or replaced with large and ornate houses, some at great expense. Reputedly the finest Georgian house ever built, Castle-coole was erected between 1788 and 1798 at a cost of some £54,000, using Portland stone brought

Crom Castle

Church at Garrison

Ashford House, Cappy

from England via Ballyshannon and the Erne waterway to Enniskillen. All of the estates were embellished with extensive tree planting in the fashionable 'English natural' manner around demesnes and deer parks, and it was the great houses, entrance gates and lodges, boundary walls, follies, quays, boat-houses, parkland and estate woodlands which brought diversity and a new kind of organisation to the countryside.

With greater stability of land tenure and agricultural improvements the quality of rural housing also improved. Stone and slate became more widespread but mud, turf and thatch continued to be used by the poorer families. Many landlords kept tight controls on the style, material and location of tenants' houses so creating local variation in settlement character. Houses were carefully sited and designed to take advantage of drainage, shelter and access. Thus in some localities

farmhouses are individually located on drumlin hills, in others they loosely cluster around a crossroads or are evenly dispersed along lanes. Some older 'clachan' type groups of houses survived in some areas. Farmyards and farm buildings continued to evolve for new purposes and the almost universal planting of trees helped to integrate farms with the surrounding countryside.

The church was another significant influence on the organisation of the countryside in the 18th and 19th centuries. Impressive stone churches were built

to designs reflecting the religious and architectural aspirations of the time. With their scale and siting, an indication of the contemporary distribution of wealth and population, they were a stimulus to further development. With churches came rectories, parochial houses, schools and halls - often the largest and finest buildings around.

Thatched house, Keenaghan

Market towns were established by landlords to serve the needs of the local communities and the trade of the estates. No two towns in Fermanagh were alike but each originally contained similar elements - a market street or square, a market house, a court house, an inn, several small shops, a pump, a cornmill, a forge and churches of different denominations. Localised textile industries - wool and linen - based on water power emerged during the 19th century and the remains of some of the larger mills are prominent in the country-side. Perhaps the most well-known mill powered the pottery at Belleek. Where suitable clay and turf for firing were found together - for example in the Arney valley - brick-making was a common supplement to farm incomes.

Belleek Pottery

With developing trade came communications by road, rail and water. Roads were progressively improved by landlords from the early 18th century onwards but particularly in the mid 19th century when, as part of famine relief, many new, often straight, roads were built. In an area so divided by water, bridges were essential, representing the most sophisticated engineering of the time and usually constructed with locally available stone. Bridge building continued well into the 20th century as the network of roads to the islands of Lough Erne was extended.

Railways and canals had a short and troubled history lacking the concentrations of population and industry to make them viable. But despite their economic problems they have left a distinctive mark on the landscape: disused lines, viaducts, station buildings and locks.

While English and Scottish settlers introduced new cultural ideas and a new economy to Fermanagh they also adapted to the local conditions. Today in the countryside there are clear contrasts between parkland scenery and land farmed in small units. Neat villages and towns have grown individually, each with its own

Brookeborough

story to tell, but even by the Second World War there was no town in Fermanagh with over 6,000 people.

Fermanagh continues to be a rural area of small towns and villages with a widely-dispersed pattern of farms. The landscape character has evolved throughout history, each period retaining something of the past and introducing something new. The chain appears complete and cultural traits, farming methods, buildings, and lines of communications all have their roots in the past.

Great-crested Grebe   photo : Ron Thompson

Fermanagh is internationally renowned for the abundance and the variety of its wildlife. Whatever the season and whatever your interest - whether serious botanist, bird-watcher or just someone who enjoys going out for a walk in the country - there is always something to catch the eye or excite the ear. The call of the curlew in spring, the flowering of the meadows in summer, the colours of the trees in autumn, the trumpeting of the whooper swans in winter - these are just some of the sights and sounds of a county steeped in wildlife.

Some thousands of years ago, much of the land was covered in dense forests of oak, but gradually the landscape that we see today was formed; bogland was cut for turf, forests were cleared and land was tilled or used for grazing animals. Although it is now a human-dominated landscape it retains many areas where wildlife is largely undisturbed.

Mountain and Moorland: The imposing summit-ridge of Cuilcagh dominates much of the county and offers spectacular views to those hardy enough to climb it. Composed of sandstone rock capped by millstone grit, the mountain rises to a height of over 2,000 feet (660 metres). On the summit and adjoining slopes rare plant species, including arctic-alpines such as creeping willow, crowberry and starry-saxifrage, are adapted to the harsh physical environment. Similarly, the ring ouzel - a rare species of thrush which looks like a blackbird with a white gorget - also makes its summer home here.

Below the slopes of Cuilcagh stretches a vast expanse of blanket bog. Here and there the apparently uniform cover of heather and sphagnum bog-mosses is broken by the patterned effect of natural pool systems - a phenomenon which is found only on intact areas of blanket bogs. In these isolated surroundings golden plover breed, and you may also catch a glimpse of one of our rarest and smallest falcons - the merlin - as it

Cuilcagh

darts over the ground in search of its prey. Other large areas of blanket bog are found to the north of Lower Lough Erne and along the border with County Tyrone on Slieve Beagh, but over much of the remainder of Fermanagh - and indeed, over much of Britain and Ireland - these wild and isolated places have been severely affected by peat-cutting or afforestation.

Upland Grasslands: On the lower slopes of Cuilcagh are areas of limestone rock extending northwards to Lower Lough Erne. This limestone escarpment is unique in Northern Ireland and it is of great importance for wildlife: a number of species occur exclusively on this type of rock material. A variety of plant communities have developed depending on slope, soil depth and drainage.

The Marlbank has flat terraces of limestone pavement

which, although not as floristically rich as the more famous pavements of the Burren in County Clare, has characteristic limestone rock grykes and associated flora in which herb robert and several species of fern dominate. Elsewhere on the shallow soils on the limestone hills, lime-loving plants, such as thyme, purging flax, mountain everlasting and quaking grass are typical. A number of rare plants can be found. Blue moor-grass, for example, is restricted to limestone rocks, and in Northern Ireland is only to be found in Fermanagh, where it is dominant over large areas of limestone grassland. Mountain avens, an alpine plant, occurs along the cliffs of Knockmore, and the very rare dense-flowered orchid has recently been discovered on Belmore Mountain. In addition, the area contains the

Mountain Everlasting, Knockmore

only known Northern Ireland breeding colony of the small blue butterfly, whose caterpillar feeds on the attractive yellow-flowered kidney vetch.

Small Blue Butterfly

Woodland and Scrub: Below the limestone escarpments of west Fermanagh the hill slopes and the steep valleys and gorges have thin and unstable soils. Difficult access has restricted farming and many remnants of native woodland have survived. On these moist, thin soils, rich in calcium, ash is the dominant tree, but other species such as birch and rowan are also frequent. The dark shapes of yew and juniper may be found on cliffs, crags and even on rocky knolls. Hazel is common below the larger trees and the ground flora is particularly rich, with a wide variety of herbs. In spring, these woods are often a mass of colour, with bluebell, wood anemone, primrose, wild garlic and a host of other flowers. The humid climate and mild winters of Fermanagh favour particularly luxuriant growths of mosses and liverworts, and a number of unusual species occur.

On the clay soils of the lowlands, most of the land is used for agriculture. However, important areas of

Broad-leaved Helleborine

woodland and scrub remain, mainly on the islands of the loughs, which are relatively inaccessible, or in estates where woodlands have been managed. On these heavier soils oak tends to dominate. The most extensive areas of this type of woodland - in Northern Ireland as well as Fermanagh - occur around Crom Castle. There, in the more open areas of parkland, many individual trees are of great age and support communities of lichens which are of interest both for their rarity value and as indicators of a woodland cover which stretches back for centuries. Lichens are especially sensitive to air pollution and thrive in the clean air of Fermanagh.

Woodland is one of the most valuable habitats for

wildlife, partly because of the number of plants present, but more importantly because of the layers of vegetation, which provide a wide range of niches for fauna, particularly insects and birds. Fermanagh woods contain a range of common breeding woodland birds, but also support more unusual species, like the wood

Correl Glen

warbler and the garden warbler, the latter occurring quite commonly on a few of the wooded islands. Insects also benefit. For example, two notable butterflies occur in Fermanagh woodlands: the rare and elusive purple hairstreak , which lays its eggs on oakbuds or twigs, is confined to a few sites in the country, while almost equally rare the striking brimstone, whose food plant as a caterpillar is the shrub, purging buckthorn, which occurs sparingly around Upper Lough Erne in areas of wet woodland and scrub along the water's edge. These wet woodlands, dominated by alder and willows, are a notable feature occupying extensive areas around all of the main loughs. Red squirrels inhabit both native and planted woodlands, while the rare and elusive pine marten can be found occasionally in large woodland tracts.

Wetland: The wet woodlands which fringe the shores of the loughs are only a small part of the total wetland habitat for which Fermanagh is justly famous. As well as the large loughs there are a host of smaller loughs dispersed across the county which contribute to the overall wetland habitat. All of these lakes are bounded to some extent by swamp, fen or wet grassland and these marginal areas provide attractive successions of

Lower Lough Erne

vegetation. Nowhere is this phenomenon better developed than on Upper Lough Erne and its surrounding lakes where open water communities with pondweeds and water lilies give way to extensive areas of swamp, with common reed and bulrush dominating.

Behind this swamp occurs species-rich fen with large sedges - often forming conspicuous tussocks - and a wide variety of herbs including flowering rush, cowbane, water parsnip and marsh pea. One of the remarkable features of Upper Lough Erne is that so many species which are rare in Ireland or Britain occur commonly around the lough: it is a botanist's paradise and ranks as one of the foremost wetland sites in the British Isles. Behind the fen there may be areas of wet, unimproved grassland itself rich in plants, including such species as quaking grass, bog pimpernel and a wide variety of sedges.

The waters and surrounding wet fields are of great value to wild animals particularly birds. On the open waters of the loughs several species of duck breed, including the scarce shoveler with its unusual broad bill. A few pairs of common scoter, which is a rarebreeding bird in Britain and Ireland, nest on the islands in Lower Lough Erne. In winter, the open waters and margins of the loughs, especially the Upper Lough, provide food and cover for a variety of wildfowl. These are mainly dabbling, or surface-feeding duck like the mallard, teal and wigeon, but also include diving duck like pochard, goldeneye and tufted duck. The whooper swan, with its distinctive trumpeting call may also be seen around the loughs. The swans migrate to Fermanagh from their breeding grounds in Iceland and winter here in internationally important numbers. The swans are frequently seen in wet pastures around the loughs, and can occur in herds of a few hundred birds in favoured areas around the Cam/Swanlinbar River and the Colebrooke River.

The low-lying wetlands in the Erne basin are also the home to very important populations of breeding wader

Snipe   *photo : Ron Thompson*

Whooper Swans, Inishmore

birds. About 800 pairs of snipe, 230 pairs of redshank, 250 pairs of curlew and 300 pairs of lapwing have bred in recent years. These waders each have their own particular habitat requirements, but in general wet grassland with sufficient cover for nests and young birds are the key criteria. Some of the islands in the Upper and Lower Loughs hold particularly dense concentrations, the security provided by isolation from the mainland being significant. The call of the curlew and the curious drumming display flight of the snipe are constant features of the area in spring and early summer.

The birds clearly benefit from the abundant invertebrate

Legalough

—23—

food resources of the wetlands. Some of the most spectacular and colourful inhabitants are dragonflies and damselfliess, which occur in large numbers around the loughs. Fermanagh is of special importance for this group of insects and 16 species have been recorded out of 22 resident Irish dragonfly species. In addition, the

Hairy Dragonfly

county is an important stronghold for several rare species including the Irish damselfly and the hairy dragonfly. It is the variety and unspoilt nature of much of the wetland habitat - whether it be large lough, small lake or peaty pool in the uplands - which makes the county so attractive to these flying insects and the many fish. In turn, the abundance of food in the water supports a good population of otters, and in more recent times, an increasing number of feral mink.

Lowland Bog: Also in the lowlands, in wet inter-drumlin hollows where peat has accumulated, are raised bogs. Originally, these were lakes but they now consist of domes of peat which have become "raised" above the water-table so that they are fed only by rainwater. As this habitat is very poor in nutrients, some plant species have developed the characteristic of supplementing their intake by catching live prey on sticky leaves, later digesting them. Otherwise the plant community is dominated by heather and sphagnum bog-mosses. A number of raised bogs occur in Fermanagh with concentrations along the valley of the Arney River. Most of these bogs have had their surface excavated for turf production, and some of the cut-over bogs are still of considerable value for wildlife - ranging from dragonflies to snipe. However, because intact lowland raised bogs are now so rare in Northern Ireland - and indeed in Europe - the more pristine sites are highly valued for conservation. Moninea Bog, near Teemore Cross, is one of the best examples in Fermanagh.

Heron's nest   *photo : Ron Thompson*

Heather

All of the various habitats which are found in Fermanagh are of value to plants and animals. Some contain more or rarer species than others, but each makes its own contribution to the overall picture; the result is a county which retains more of its natural heritage than any other in Northern Ireland and which has international renown for its overall wildlife interest.

Dairy Herd, Aghavoory

Farmers, and other workers of the land, have made the Fermanagh countryside - its fields, hedges, ditches, woods, houses, sheds and lanes. Field to field differences in farm practice - drainage, grazing regime, crops and livestock - pattern the landscape, adding to local and regional variation in character. And, bordering the fields, the bogs, mountains and loughs complete the picture of rural Fermanagh. The continued success of farming and the maintenance of existing rural communities are crucial for the economy and fundamental to the management of the land resource together with all its wildlife and historical interests.

Virtually all of the land has been farmed in some manner, at some time in history. Before the advent of prehistoric farming all but the hill summits and lakes were clothed in a dense forest of oak, ash and elm. Even as late as the 18th century woodland was extensive. Now most of the native woodland has been cleared and in 1990 only about 4% of Fermanagh supported semi-natural woodland.

Fermanagh farmers have inherited a tradition of cattle rearing; in the past the freedom to move with the cattle was highly valued and a system of seasonal grazing of the uplands, or booleying, was widespread. With 18th century land improvements arable farming became more important, particularly in the east of the county, but Fermanagh's climate and soils never really favoured arable cropping.

By the beginning of the 19th century most of the population depended on potatoes and milk for three-quarters of their food and on oats for the remainder. With the success of potato harvests the population doubled in fifty years but crop failures between 1845 and 1847 caused famine and disaster. Subsequent population decline led to a gradual change in the rural economy and a move back to livestock.

Potatoes had become established as an indispensable crop, including fodder for some 7,500 horses and a remarkable 4,500 asses and mules present in the latter half of the 19th century. As well as potatoes, wheat, oats and flax were grown, particularly on the better soils of east Fermanagh. In these areas large-scale tillage techniques were practised with a continuing dependence on draft animals - by 1930 only 7 tractors were registered in Fermanagh. However, on some smaller farms spade cultivation remained important. The area of crops increased during the World Wars but by 1990 less than 1% of the land was arable, the main crops being oats, potatoes and barley.

Pigs and poultry were also important in the largely subsistence economy of the 19th century but production has fluctuated considerably in more recent times and is now becoming increasingly confined to a small number of specialist producers.

Cattle, and to a lesser extent sheep, are today the backbone of the agricultural industry. In the modern market economy, commodities need to be produced where they benefit from natural advantages and in Fermanagh well-managed, highly productive grassland favours livestock. The cattle population has practically doubled over the past 150 years and of some 3,000 farm businesses now in Fermanagh some 57% are beef cattle and sheep while 40% are principally dairying. Suckler cow herds are very important with over 40,000 suckler cows compared to 27,000 dairy cows in 1985.

The contrast between east and west is still evident in the farmed landscape. Broadly speaking, west of the lakes, there is more rough grazing, more hay production on meadowland, and more rush-infested fields on poorly- drained, difficult soils. East of the lakes grass is produced more intensively and there is generally greater opportunity for more progressive farming in profitable farm businesses (See Fig. 1, Appendix).

In spring, as soon as ground conditions become suitable, cattle are turned out to graze and field operations such as manure, slurry and fertilizer spreading begin. Between May and September grass is cut for silage in one, two or perhaps even three cuttings. Although haymaking is widespread, the quantity won is very much related to the weather from summer to summer and grass silage is the predominant winter fodder. Meadows, often unsuitable for heavy

West Fermanagh: Haymaking, Roogagh Bridge

East Fermanagh: Dairying, Colebrooke Valley

....It is more difficult to make general statements about the agricultural land use of Fermanagh than of any other county in the province....Everywhere there are irregular variations of farm size and practice, soil type and drainage conditions. One townland can differ radically from the next, and one farm from its neighbour; even different fields on the same farm can be strikingly dissimilar. The chief characteristic of farming in Fermanagh is the extreme diversity over limited areas, in fact, diversity within uniformity....

Cruickshank and McHugh 1963 [4]

machinery, are traditional for haymaking, the light coverage of mixed grasses being won by hand or light machinery in only a few days if the weather is right.

Traditional methods of lapping and ruck building can still be seen in west Fermanagh but generally elsewhere the hay is baled straight from the swathe.

Grazing of sheep or cattle continues for as long as autumn conditions permit, the animals being gradually moved closer to home or to fields selected for over-wintering. Rush topping is carried out annually, usually in late summer, and often the rushes are baled for use as winter bedding. Turf is cut, won and brought home in as short a time as possible in late spring and early summer. One can witness a procession of tractors and trailers carrying the turf home in a race against time as a frontal depression approaches from the Atlantic. Family involvement is traditional in the summertime activities of peat cutting and haymaking.

Upper Lough Erne

Hay meadow, Screenagh Valley

The use of the land is very important for its wildlife and scenic interest. Although much of the farmland has been improved by drainage and fertilizer there are still wet meadows, rough pastures and lough margins which are farmed at a low intensity and support a great variety of plants, insects and birds. In early summer it is a common sight to see the colourful spectacle of a flower-rich meadow with hay-rattle, ragged robin, ox-eye daisy and a host of orchids. The meadows are also the home of the corncrake, with its rasping call. Formerly widespread over the British Isles, the corncrake has declined alarmingly in recent years, partly because haymaking has become less popular. Early cutting for silage can destroy nests and young birds. Fermanagh is now its last refuge in Northern Ireland, and its survival

will to some extent depend on the continuation of haymaking.

Despite the overwhelming extent of grassland, visually it is thick hedges and groups of trees which tend to dominate the rolling drumlin countryside. Fields are often very small and almost everywhere hedges mark the field boundaries. Hedges are generally thick and overgrown with a great variety of trees and shrubs, mostly hawthorn, ash, blackthorn, willow, alder, and

Hedges near Drummully

holly. In addition to controlling stock, their food and shelter has been appreciated over the years. They often contain many old herbal cures and the hazel nuts, blackberries, raspberries and strawberries have added variety to the country diet. Some of the older hedges, such as those marking townland boundaries, may be ancient field boundaries containing fragments of the woodland which covered the lowlands, their species

richness and varied floral undercover derived from that woodland.

As the drumlin slopes begin to flatten out the hedges are left behind and open drains or sheughs divide the flat meadowland. Many of these drains and ditches have thriving wetland plants and around the Upper Lough, in particular, they contain some rare plant species.

Stone walls or ditches are used as field boundaries in localities where the outcrop of limestone or sandstone is easily accessible. While particularly evident along the limestone outcrops of west Fermanagh they are limited in extent elsewhere - only 2% of all field boundaries are stone walls. However the walls highlight the rock variety and add to the local landscape

Stone wall, Knockmore

character. In the uplands earth banks and ditches with scattered thorn and whin bushes are more typical.

Whether moving uphill onto the mountain plateaus or down into the valley bottoms, intensive farming gives way to bog; either blanket bog on the hills or raised bog on the lowland. Bog provides limited rough grazing but in the past it was most valued for turf. On the slopes of the uplands and on pockets of better soils, cultivation has advanced and retreated through history - influenced by climatic conditions, farming techniques and population pressure. Farming in these marginal conditions in the 19th century depended on small gardens cultivated for potatoes and vegetables, grazing of cattle on the mountain and cutting turf for fuel.

Turf cutting continues today and less than half the upland blanket peat remains undisturbed by past or

Turf cutting, Lough Navar

present activity. The lines of old turf banks and the stacks of freshly-cut peat are traditional features of the landscape but extensive areas of bare and degraded peat left by mechanised peat extraction are an eyesore and a threat to wildlife.

Within the last thirty years the uplands have begun to be once again mantled with trees but the scene is not as of old. About one tenth of Fermanagh has been planted with Sitka spruce and other coniferous trees. Such forests are a new element in the upland landscape: the rows of uniform trees, the straight-lined edges of plantations and the covering of the natural topography are, by many, considered to be an intrusion into the wilderness. Whilst the forests introduce new habitats for wildlife, particularly woodland birds and small mammals, they also replace the open moorland habitat favoured by less common wader birds and birds of prey, such as the golden plover, dunlin and merlin. However, by enlightened management, foresters can design the plantations to integrate with the landscape and, by selective planting, can ensure that the better wildlife habitats are retained. Forest roads, car parks and footpaths have provided public access to the uplands affording, for example at Lough Navar Forest, magnificent views across the county.

The lowland bogs have a similar history of use for turf and seasonal grazing of stock but the extent of bogs has been considerably reduced by progressive turf cutting and reclamation for agriculture. Less than 10% of the area of all such bogs survive in their natural state and many are a patchwork of different vegetation types. Within a small area sphagnum bog can be adjacent to an emergent woodland of birch, a plantation of spruce, a reclaimed field of ryegrass, a rushy pasture or a hay meadow.

Carrigans Forest

Farmhouse, Church Hill

Conservation Today

Conservation aims to protect the environmental assets of the countryside, to enhance its qualities wherever possible and to ensure the wise and sustainable use of its resources. These objectives go hand in hand with the promotion of enjoyment of the countryside so that local people and visitors may better appreciate the value of their environment. Conservation does not necessarily oppose development but instead it tries to ensure that development leads to an improved environment and long-term benefits to the community. Fermanagh people have a heritage of conservation: traditional farming, use of land and water, buildings and communications, by necessity worked with the natural environment, slowly and surely making best use of limited resources. The landscapes and wildlife of Fermanagh are a tribute to this approach.

Fermanagh as a whole has some very special qualities:

* the outstanding landscapes of the lakeland, mountains and the limestone scarps; the inter-relation of water bodies and farmland in the countryside;

* the traditional character of farming with its close association with natural habitats - streams, woodland, hedges, meadows and hill pasture - and the heritage of traditional farm practices;

* the abundance, quality and international importance of wildlife habitats, in particular the lough shores, wetlands, woodlands and limestone areas;

* the high quality of freshwater environments of rivers and loughs providing exceptional fishing and attractive landscape features;

* the remarkable limestone caves around Cuilcagh and Boho which are amongst the longest, deepest and most exciting caves in Ireland;

* the richness and diversity of archaeological sites including some of the best examples in Northern Ireland of megalithic monuments, Early Christian religious sites and settlements and Plantation castles;

* the wide variety of traditional building styles and locations including; grand estate houses, estate buildings, lodges, farms and farmyards of all sizes, many occupied and adjusted to suit present day requirements; churches, schools, mills and bridges of historical and architectural interest;

* the occasional small town or village with many traditional buildings retaining its individual character, role and identity and almost hidden in its local rural setting;

* the county town of Enniskillen with its historic island location, designated Conservation Area and service facilities providing a natural focus for tourism;

* the people themselves with their strong local loyalties and individual character; and

* the opportunities for carefree, varied and challenging recreation in a high-quality, uncrowded, rural environment.

Looked at in more detail, each area of Fermanagh has its own special landscape character and particular features of interest. Part B describes sixteen distinct landscapes within Fermanagh and summarises their special conservation interest and issues.

FERMANAGH LANDSCAPES

1. The Erne Lakeland.
2. The Sillees Valley.
3. The Knockmore Scarpland.
4. The Lough Navar and Ballintempo Uplands.
5. The Garrison Lowlands.
6. The Lough Macnean Valley.
7. Cuilcagh and Marlbank.
8. The Arney Lowlands.

9. Slieve Russel, Derrylin and Kinawley.
10. Newtownbutler and Rosslea Lowlands.
11. Carnrock and Cooneen Hills.
12. Colebrooke and Tempo River Valley.
13. Topped and Brougher Mountain Uplands.
14. Ballinamallard and Irvinestown Lowlands.
15. Glendarragh and Bannagh River Valleys.
16. Croagh and Garvary River.

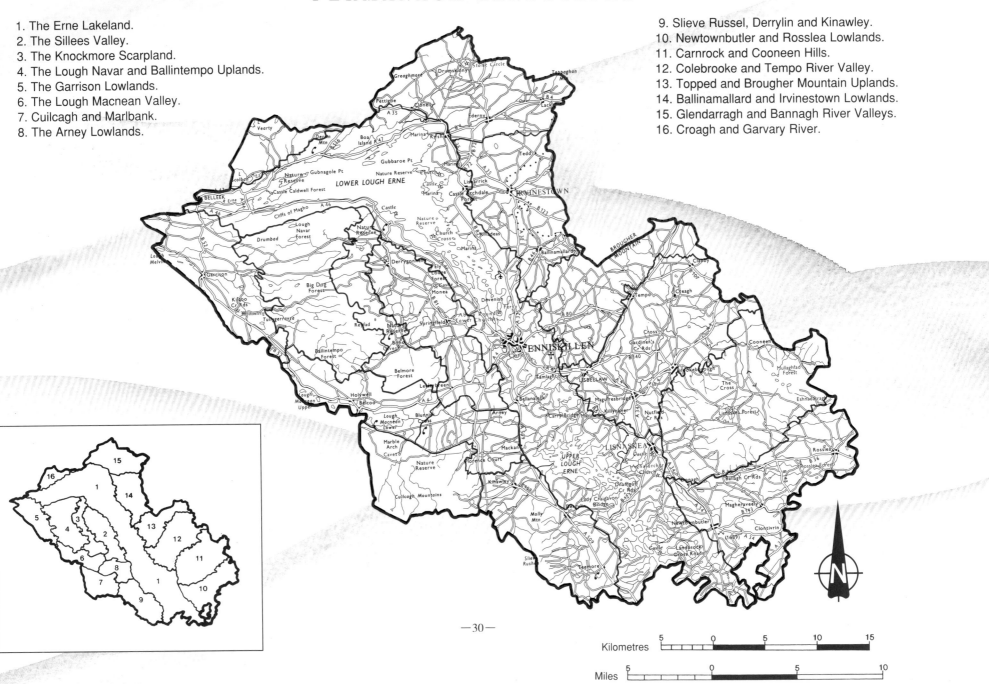

—30—

Kilometres

Miles

The people of Fermanagh naturally aspire to the high standard of living and good economic livelihood which has been achieved elsewhere in Western Europe. Whilst, on one side of the coin the peripheral location and 'less-favoured' agriculture may be seen as problems, on the other, the unspoilt and uncrowded countryside is a positive attraction. In recent years European Community and United Kingdom government policy and funding has recognised some of these problems and has sought to take advantage of some of the opportunities.

The countryside has been changing: farming has become both more extensive and more intensive, with smaller holdings becoming economically marginal; forestry has spread across uplands and on to lowlands; tourism facilities have been developed along lough shores and in the wider countryside; population has been declining in some areas and housing has been modernised or replaced by new roadside dwellings; and towns and villages have developed as local resid ential and service centres. The changes will doubtlessly continue.

New initiatives have emerged which place greater emphasis on the need for programmes of integrated development. Agriculture, tourism, local industry and conservation are so closely associated that their promotion cannot be considered independently. Agricultural policy has developed a strong environmental component aimed at countryside conservation. Attractive farmland, heritage, wildlife and fisheries are essential to tourism, whilst small towns and local industry provide alternative employment and income for rural communities.

In Fermanagh there are opportunities to develop agriculture and forestry, to exploit tourism and to promote public enjoyment of the countryside. Such development and promotion could bring major economic benefits but this should not be at the expense of the existing environmental assets - the landscape, wildlife and heritage features. Sustainable development and conservation <u>can</u> be achieved by co-ordination, co-operation and consultation between the people, the District Council and all the government agencies involved and suitable mechanisms for this need to be created.

Devenish

An Agenda For Conservation

a. LANDSCAPES

The landscapes of Fermanagh are remarkably beautiful. The farmed countryside, lakeland, limestone scarp and mountain scenery combine to make a dramatic impact, unique and stimulating. All of the landscapes deserve to be treated with care and their assets managed for the benefit of future generations.

It is a matter for discussion whether or not some of the most beautiful landscapes deserve to be recognised nationally by their designation as Areas of Outstanding Natural Beauty (AONBs). Designation would give a priority to the conservation of their special character, to the promotion of their beauty and wildlife and heritage interest and to the provision of facilities so that they can be more fully enjoyed and appreciated. In AONBs central and local government, local people and voluntary groups can work together to establish management objectives, to develop policies and to make proposals for the conservation and enjoyment of the countryside.

The Department of the Environment suggests that all or parts of two areas in particular merit designation as Areas of Outstanding Natural Beauty:-

'Erne Lakeland' - including Upper and Lower Lough Erne and Enniskillen (Special Landscape 1); and

Doocharn Island

'Fermanagh Caveland' - including the limestone scarplands of Knockmore and Marble Arch, the Lough Macnean Valley and the afforested uplands between Lough Navar and Ballintempo (Special Landscapes 3, 4, 6 and 7)(see map on Page 30).

Knockmore

b. FARMING

Farming is crucial to the local economy, it maintains the landscape and helps protect the wildlife interest of the countryside. Soil and climatic conditions in Fermanagh favour grassland production and livestock. Successful, profitable farming has maintained the local population which in turn has supported local services

Making silage

and businesses in towns and villages. Recently many small farms have not provided an adequate income and some have had to be incorporated into larger farm businesses or sold for forestry. Medium and larger-sized farms are increasingly faced with intensification as a means of maintaining income levels. The social and environmental implications of declining farm incomes are serious: rural depopulation; dereliction of traditional housing; ageing population structure; closure of local services and businesses; abandonment of traditional agricultural practices; rush-infestation and scrub encroachment and loss of detailed landscape structure.

Additional support for the farm industry and rural

communities needs to be considered. Environmentally sensitive farming, diversification, tourism and forestry are amongst options which can be explored.

c. WILDLIFE

Fermanagh contains some of the best areas of natural habitats in Northern Ireland and some of these are rare in a United Kingdom or European Community context. About one third of the land area has not been improved for agriculture or forestry and can be considered to have a semi-natural vegetation of particular value for wildlife (Fig. 1, Appendix). In 28 nature reserves wildlife is specifically protected but outside these areas wildlife depends on the use of the land by farmers and other landowners (Fig. 2, Appendix). Particular threats are

Bluebells

the clearance of woodland and scrub, the extensive cutting of peat bogs, the drainage of both wetlands and watercourses, the reclamation and improvement of wet meadows and rough grazing, the pollution and enrichment of water courses and the removal of ancient hedgerows. To a large extent, the notable wildlife habitats of Fermanagh have been lost from other parts of the United Kingdom through agricultural improvement and other developments. There should be an ongoing programme of assessment in order to evaluate the scientific value of the county and monitor any changes: the best sites will be declared Areas of Special Scientific Interest.

Farmers should be encouraged to continue the conservation and improvement of wildlife habitats on their farms. In many cases habitats can be protected or enhanced without loss of income or inconvenience to farmers and other landowners. Where farmers experience a loss of income or incur expenditure through such conservation management they should be compensated. Payments may be possible from the Department of Agriculture and the Department of the Environment under various grant schemes, such as the designation of Environmentally Sensitive Areas, the Corncrake Grant

Scheme 1990 and various tree planting grants.

Upper and Lower Lough Erne are of particular wildlife significance but in all areas nature conservation interests should be considered as important factors relating to development.

d. WOODLAND AND FORESTRY

Fermanagh, with 15% of land area under woodland and forest, is the most wooded county in Northern Ireland. Two-thirds of this is recent coniferous plantation but there are also significant areas of semi-natural and estate woodlands (Fig. 3, Appendix).

Trees grow well in Fermanagh, especially in the more sheltered locations, and natural scrub colonisation occurs on under-grazed pasture and cut-over bogs. Thick, overgrown hedges and groups of trees around

Lough shore, Castle Caldwell

farm buildings are characteristic of all the lowlands and add to the impression of a wooded countryside. Many woodlands are important wildlife habitats and make a particular contribution to the landscape. The trees on the shoreline and islands of Lough Erne are distinctive features and also serve to screen shoreline development. However the wildlife value of established woodland is diminished by widespread grazing of livestock and general absence of management. Estate woodlands are often in a poor condition. Further encouragement should be given to woodland management and tree planting.

Forestry makes a widespread impact on landscape and has reduced certain upland wildlife habitats. However Forest Service policy now favours lowland rather than

Forestry, Dooraa

upland sites for further expansion and this policy is supported by conservation interests. Forest conservation

guidelines take account of landscape, wildlife and heritage in forest design and management and 13 Forest Nature Reserves have been declared. Recreation facilities have been developed at several sites, for example the Lough Navar scenic drive and Castle Caldwell visitor centre and much of the Ulster Way and many short footpaths are also provided by Forest Service. These facilities add significantly to the overall recreation resources of Fermanagh.

e. HERITAGE

Archaeological monuments and historic buildings are a distinctive feature of Fermanagh and add greatly to the interest of the countryside. Particularly well-represented

Devenish

are Neolithic megalithic tombs, Bronze Age burials and stone circles, Early Christian churches and settlements and Plantation castles and estates. Eleven sites are in State Care and are open to the public. A further 126 monuments are Scheduled thus requiring prior notification of any damaging operations. The Department is concerned to protect <u>all</u> historic monuments and the work of Scheduling is ongoing (Fig. 4, Appendix).

Belle Isle

There are 332 Listed buildings which should not be altered without permission of the Department and some of these may be eligible for grant aid. Listed buildings range from the great houses of Castle Coole and Florence Court, which are maintained and presented to the public by the National Trust, to more modest houses and other buildings in towns, villages and the countryside. The Conservation Area in Enniskillen aims to protect and enhance the character of the town centre (Fig. 5, Appendix).

Most historic monuments and buildings are in private ownership and rely for their care upon the good sense and respect shown by their owners. Advice on their conservation is available from the Department of the Environment. The heritage of Fermanagh is a major attraction for visitors. Access, facilities and information should be improved to enable greater appreciation and enjoyment without damage to privacy or property.

f. HOUSING AND DEVELOPMENT

Apart from the county town, Enniskillen, and a number of widely dispersed small towns and villages, a high proportion of people live within the Fermanagh countryside.

Often the older rural buildings have attractive settings, in harmony with the local topography and associated

House near Ely Lodge

with mature broad-leaf trees. But many such buildings provide a standard of accommodation below that now normally expected and are located away from the service utilities along county roads. Thus it is apparent, in many areas, that older, small and remote houses are being replaced by new housing close to the roads. These new buildings often lack traditional design details and are usually larger. Screening, when planted, in many cases takes the form of exotic conifers which do not blend with surrounding hedges and woodland. In some instances, where houses are located to give panoramic views, they themselves are highly visible and dominant in the landscape. However, the undulating relief and tree cover of the lowlands can often absorb housing and other development satisfactorily so long as careful attention is given to location, siting and design and to the treatment of boundaries. The Department intends to prepare a statutory plan for Fermanagh and has appointed consultants to advise on a Rural Development Strategy.

g. MINERAL WORKINGS

The limestones of Fermanagh have been an important source of building stone through the ages and extraction continues today at a number of sites,

principally for aggregates but also for cement and magnesia limestone. A dolerite dyke outcrop at Doraville is quarried for roadstone, and sands and gravels are worked locally around Derrylin and Tempo. Peat is cut widely but mostly for domestic consumption. Traditionally cutting was by hand but in recent years mechanised extraction has become more evident, with significant local environmental impacts.

Quarry near Belcoo

The quarrying of limestone at Knockninny and on the escarpments of west Fermanagh near Belcoo and west of Enniskillen unfortunately coincides with areas of particular scenic beauty. They provide some examples of the kind of inherent conflict which can arise between conservation and the perceived need to extract rock in such landscapes. There is a challenge for the future in dealing with both problems of expansion and landscape restoration. In east Fermanagh quarries tend to be less obtrusive.

Fermanagh's landscapes together present a comprehensive and varied range of resources and opportunities for leisure pursuits and countryside enjoyment. The lakes, rivers and lough-shore areas accommodate a multiplicity of water sport, fishing, heritage and wildlife interests while, in the countryside in general, walking, caving and horse-riding pursuits are being developed in combination with scenic enjoyment and other more specialised interests. In recent years parking places, viewpoints, scenic routes, picnic sites, marinas, a Country Park, footpaths and many other facilities have been provided. Development has included hotels, chalets, guest-houses, restaurants and caravan and camping sites (Fig.3, Appendix).

Fermanagh District Council has been a major promoter of recreation and tourism. The Department of the Environment, Department of Agriculture and Department of Economic Development, have given support in the provision of facilities and funds. Private companies and individuals have also contributed through, for example, cruiser hire, guest-houses and restaurants. Voluntary bodies, and in particular the National Trust, have demonstrated how conservation of the national heritage can provide enjoyment for many and create major tourist attractions.

Consultants for Fermanagh District Council have identified a number of specific developments which would strengthen the overall tourism attraction of Fermanagh and the Council, together with private interests and public funding, is seeking to implement the recommendations.

Government policy recognises that tourism and leisure pursuits are likely to make an increasing contribution to the local economy and grant-aid is offered, through a variety of sources, for approved projects. However, it is also clear, that the major tourist resources - the countryside, loughs, waterways, wildlife and heritage - are vulnerable to insensitive or conflicting developments. The full potential of the countryside and loughs to attract, accommodate and satisfy visitors may not be achieved without co-ordinated management. Thus, for those areas where opportunities and pressure for development are greatest and where environments are also most sensitive, such as around the shores of Lough Erne, there is a need for management strategies agreed in full consultation with all other interested parties.

Lower Lough Erne

Part B

SPECIAL LANDSCAPES

....Nobody inhabited these small humps of land,

each flung on the water's surface like a brilliant

arras woven with purple loosestrife and marigold-

goldins, strings of sovereigns and the majestic

standard-bearers of golden-rod. A sweet scent

suffused from hemp agrimony, an irresistable lure

to the gaudiest butterflies, who fluttered as though

drawn by magnets to the raspberry-and-cream

groves. There were reed labyrinths where the

black scoter went to breed, and desert island

shores turned by sandpipers into excited play-

grounds. Birdsong sounded like the music of

paradise and wings whirred on glissando flights

from sunshine to shadow, in and out of the woods.

From surrounding drumlins the wood-pigeon let

fall his billing notes, and as we made for home, the

throbbing of the nightjar filled the air with a

mechanical, insistent purr....

Robert Harbinson [5]

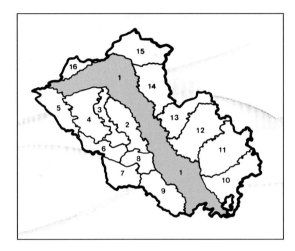

Lower Lough Erne

Landscape Character

Running like a thread of silver through the heart of Fermanagh is the River Erne and its two great lakes, Upper and Lower Lough Erne. In the middle of these, literally, Enniskillen is the hub of the county. The loughs, rivers, valleys and roads all radiate, like spokes of a wheel, from the town at the crossing point on the Erne. The loughs divide, by making land communications difficult, yet unite, by providing the historic focus of activity. Each lough has a very different landscape character and moods change from day to day and season to season. The River Erne flows into the south of Upper Lough Erne, links the two lakes by a tortuous route through Enniskillen and then, after passing through Lower Lough Erne, flows west to enter the sea in Donegal Bay - a river to which Fermanagh owes much of its individuality.

Lower Lough Erne

Of the two lakes the Lower Lough is the more dramatic; its waters spread from the myriad of islands near Enniskillen to lap around the bold escarpment of the Magho cliffs. The lough, larger than any in England, Scotland or Wales, stretches in a vast crescent shape for almost 20 miles from Enniskillen to Rosscor and at its widest is some five miles across. Formed in a deep glacial trough, the lineation of shores, islands, promontories and bays reflects the direction of ice-flow of the last Ice Age.

Along the southern shore and towards the western end of the lough, ice-scoured limestones and ancient quartzite rocks of Donegal, make a harsher landscape with prominent rocky scarps and hills. The stepped escarpment of Cullen Hill above Ely Lodge and the sheer Magho cliffs are distinct from the low streamlined ridges of Boa Island and Castle Caldwell. The southern shore of the lough, below Magho, is exposed and has boulder-strewn beaches backed by an almost continuous fringe of alder woodland. Only a narrow strip of farmland lies between the shore and the scarp slopes.

The River Erne leaves the lough inconspicuously at Rosscor and despite the massive discharge, its valley is small and hidden. Belleek at the western extremity of Fermanagh, only five miles from the Atlantic, is now the terminus of Erne navigation and it is there that water levels are controlled and water is used downstream for the generation of hydroelectric power. No rivers cut through the escarpment to the south of the Lower Lough but in the softer drumlin country of the eastern shorelines the Termon, Bannagh, Kesh, and Ballinamallard Rivers wander into hidden bays. The Termon and Bannagh drain through extensive areas of marsh and fen into the relatively sheltered, isolated reach of Lower Lough Erne north of Boa Island. There, and amongst islands and promontories near Castle Caldwell and Castle Archdale, reed beds flourish in the enclosed bays.

Towards Enniskillen, as the Lower Lough narrows into the channels of the River Erne, high drumlin hills begin to dominate the scene, forming wooded islands and long promontories. The town of Enniskillen itself is built on a drumlin island in the middle of the River Erne channel.

Upper Lough Erne
In comparison to the wide, open Lower Lough, the

Upper Lough Erne

Upper Lough has a small-scale, intricate landscape in which the main River Erne channel splits and joins, widens and narrows around islands of varying shape and size. Beads of low-lying interconnected drumlins stretch across the lough from east to west, providing connections such as at Craigavon Bridge or Derryvore. Views vary from closed-in bays and inlets, to wider reaches of open water scattered with low islands, the shores thickly wooded and the surrounding drumlin hills divided by a dense patchwork of fields and hedges. Between drumlins, yet isolated from the main lough, are numerous small loughs each with fringing reed beds, carr woodland and an occasional ancient crannog.

From Enniskillen to Belle Isle the waters of the River Erne are confined to channels that weave between drumlin islands and promontories, opening into bays which flood interdrumlin hollows such as Tamlaght Bay, and squeezing between steep drumlin banks as at Carry Bridge. The slow flowing waters of the Erne are joined by the Arney and Sillees Rivers, the major tributaries which drain the uplands to the west. The scene is varied with isolated farms, ruined churches and wooded parklands of estates.

Inisherk

South of Belle Isle is the widest area of Upper Lough Erne but the expanse of water is broken by low islands, small in scale, their impact strengthened by dense woodland canopies. The surrounding shorelines are low-lying; the Colebrooke River joining the lough from the north and the Cladagh or Swanlinbar River from the south, occupy broad marshy floodplains.

Continuing upstream south of Trasna Island, the lough again narrows, and islands, bays and headlands increase in scale as small hills rise steeply from the water's edge. These sheltered bays among tall, wooded, interconnected drumlins are more remote and less frequented than other parts of the lough. Eventually Upper Lough Erne terminates in a chaotic tangle of lough, river, marsh and land at the confluence of the Erne, Finn and Woodford Rivers.

The only prominent landmark in the whole of this twenty miles or more of waterways on Upper Lough Erne is the singular hill of Knockninny which rises mysteriously from the surrounding, half-flooded, drumlin plain. From its slopes the views of the lough are breathtaking. The hill is an outlier of the Upper Limestone escarpments to the south and west, its lough-shore location making it an important source of building stone.

Lough and Lough Shores

For both Upper and Lower Lough Erne it is the detail of island and shoreline margins which contributes much to the local scene. In the sheltered bays of Upper Lough Erne and to a lesser extent in Lower Lough Erne there are broad reed beds of varying colour and height giving way inland to a succession of swamp, fen and carr woodland. A strip of damp grassland, seasonally flooded, frequently fringes the shores and cattle graze and wander into the shallow waters to drink, retreating behind tall uncut hedges for shelter from wind and rain. Stony beaches are found in more exposed locations. However it is the fringing woodlands which characterise much of the shoreline and for birds the loughs, fen, swampy grassland, meadows and woods are

a paradise abundant with food and shelter. The waters themselves represent some of the best coarse fishing in Northern Ireland. Lough and river water quality is sensitive to enrichment with high nutrient loadings from industrial and domestic effluents and run-off from agricultural land throughout the Erne catchment.

Agricultural land around the loughs varies considerably from good quality grassland in large fields, to rushy pasture in very small fields surrounded by tall hedge-rows. Grassland quality varies from field to field and from farm to farm but generally the better land is around Enniskillen, extending towards Kesh, Newtownbutler, Church Hill and Arney. High water levels in the loughs are a major constraint to agricultural improvement along the lough shores. Dairy and suckler cow herds are important, alongside beef cattle.

Where old estates adjoin the shorelines, for example, Crom, Belle Isle and Castle Coole in Upper Lough Erne and Ely Lodge, Castle Caldwell and Castle Archdale in Lower Lough Erne, trees, woodland and forest have a major impact. The larger areas of broad-leaf woodlands on some islands and around the Crom estate preserve some of the best examples of native oak woodland in

Lower Lough Erne

....My joy in these trips on the lake did not come from fishing, but from merely sailing in and out of the creeks and inlets. Fermanagh spread out before me in a jigsaw of islands. At sundown, the lakes became millponds of shining ormolu-varnish, enriched with sparkling inlaid patterns where the engine frothed the wake behind us....

Robert Harbinson [6]

Northern Ireland. However, many estate woodlands are neither actively managed nor in good condition. Commercial constraints of modern forest plantations mean it is not easy to match the elegant plantings of 18th and 19th century estate landscapes. Elsewhere, many large farms, often sited on high drumlins, are surrounded by groups of mixed trees and fine individual trees in hedges or open field, a pleasing adjunct to the well-managed grassland.

Island landscapes tend to be either open and treeless, like Dernish, or densely wooded, like the adjacent Inish Rath. They are most famous for their historic remains which stretch from one end of Fermanagh to the other. Old abbeys, churches and graveyards on the islands and shores, and the many castles and the great houses together span 1,400 years of history.

Settlement

The lough-shore scene extends into the heart of Enniskillen linking the town with the lakeland. The two channels of the Erne and the adjacent small loughs give the old County town an exceptional landscape setting taken advantage of in parkland and open spaces. The 17th century settlement pattern is retained in the single

Enniskillen Castle

street which runs the full length of the island connecting the bridges at either end. Many buildings are of historic or architectural interest and the older street frontages are, as a whole, uninterrupted by recent development. Newer suburbs and industrial sites sprawl out over adjacent drumlins fragmented by water channels, bays, islands and by farmed and wooded slopes.

Lisnaskea, Kesh and Belleek are the other main settlements around the loughs, though there are several small villages, like Church Hill and Lisnarrick, and other loosely-clustered groups of houses. Lisnaskea is an ancient settlement site and its present layout and buildings reflect its role as an important market town in the 18th and 19th centuries. Kesh is little more than a single street of houses at the bridging point of the Kesh River, a junction with routes to Enniskillen, Omagh, Castlederg, Donegal and Ballyshannon. Belleek, most famous for its pottery and trout fishing, is an old estate town with a broad market street bordered by small shops and houses. The towns provide local services; they are

Smith's Strand

central in community life and important for the development of tourist facilities.

Outside of the towns and villages, rural houses have traditionally avoided the lough shore because of flooding. Older houses are more often located on drumlin slopes in sheltered positions. Traditional dwellings vary from 2 or $2\frac{1}{2}$ storey houses on large farms or small estates to small, single storey houses with thatched roofs. New dwellings are common either as replacements or as new development in attractive lakeland settings, particularly in accessible locations within ten miles of Enniskillen. New housing often occupies prominent positions commanding panoramic views. Many islands have been settled in the past but most of those without bridge connections are now not permanently occupied.

Recreation and Tourism

The Erne Lakeland is a popular holiday destination and has good facilities for land and water-based recreation.

Accommodation is provided in hotels, guest-houses, caravan parks, self-catering chalets and aboard cruisers. Marinas and other facilities are dispersed around the two loughs from Belleek in the west to Crom Castle and the new Ballyconnell Canal link in the south, with the greatest concentration of development between Kesh and Enniskillen. Lough-shore developments can directly impinge on important wildlife habitats and be visually intrusive. Access to the lough is provided at a large number of public sites with car parking, boat launching, mooring, fishing and picnic facilities. Several artificial beaches have been created. At Castle Archdale Country Park, Castle Caldwell, Tully Castle, Ely Lodge Forest and Crom Castle, there are larger areas of land open for public access. Historic monuments and buildings open to the public are popular to visitors.

Enniskillen has now an international flavour on the streets as at different times of the year the fishermen from many countries come to catch their first trout or to compete in coarse fishing festivals. Conflicts can arise in the use of the lough and lough shores for these various pursuits without harming the quality of the water, landscapes and wildlife habitats.

Conservation Interest and Issues

In the space available, it is impossible to do justice to the wealth of conservation interests and complex management issues in the Erne Lakeland. A fuller account must await a later study.

LANDSCAPE Lakeland scenery of outstanding quality and highly valued: Tremendous variety in the interplay of land and water, the informality of fringing wetland and woodland, farmland and estates.

FARMING Good quality grassland on better-drained drumlin hills interspersed with wet meadows, bogs and marsh in the hollows: Farm improvements evident: Dairy herds, suckler cows, beef cattle and sheep: Diversification into tourism activities.

WILDLIFE Wildlife of the loughs, lough shores and islands and in wetland, woodland and meadow habitats is of national and international importance: Loughs support breeding wildfowl and provide winter feeding for migrants including whooper swans: Wet grasslands around the loughs important for breeding wader birds: Nature reserves at Castle Caldwell, Castle Archdale, Magho, Naan Island, Crom Castle and Reilly and Gole Woods and Namanfin Island.

WOODLAND AND FORESTRY Natural woodland prominent on the lough shores and islands but old estate plantations and more recent afforestation also characteristic: Estate woodlands at Crom Castle, Belle Isle, Castle Coole, Castle Hume, Ely Lodge, Manor House, and Castle Archdale: Forestry mostly confined to old estates at Castle Caldwell, Castle Archdale and Ely Lodge: Highly visible forestry spills over the Cliffs of Magho from Lough Navar: Forest Service provide a high standard of recreation facilities.

HERITAGE Islands and lough shores particularly rich in Early Christian monuments and the group of ecclesiastical sites is the most important in Northern Ireland: Raths in the surrounding drumlin countryside and crannogs in many small loughs: Ruins of castles of Plantation period: Estates and country houses: Sites in State Care include, Devenish, White Island, Inishmacsaint, Tully Castle, Enniskillen Castle, Castlebalfour and Aghalurcher Church: Estates at Castle Coole and Crom Castle managed by the National Trust: Numerous Listed buildings ranging from estate properties and churches to small houses and bridges.

HOUSING AND DEVELOPMENT Enniskillen, the major town, is attractive and of great historic interest: Smaller centres at Lisnaskea, Kesh and Belleek: Lisnaskea, historic town and an important growth centre: Belleek renowned for its pottery: Rural settlement includes many traditional buildings of estates and farms: High density of derelict buildings: Replacement dwellings a feature of accessible lough-shore and roadside locations: Hotels, restaurants, marinas, chalets and caravan parks often have prominent lough-shore sites.

MINERAL WORKING Prominent limestone quarries at Knockninny, Lenaghan and Banagher: Limestone also quarried at Lough Scolban: Quarry in dolerite dyke at Doraville near Killadeas.

RECREATION AND TOURISM Wide variety of tourist and recreation facilities focused on the loughs: Provision for cruising, fishing and water sports: Open public access to Country and Forest Parks: Historic monuments and buildings open to public: Local services and accommodation in towns and villages: Access to lough shore tends to be concentrated at nodes: Most of the land adjoining the lough and the islands is in private ownership: Some conflicts in recreation use.

2 THE SILLEES VALLEY

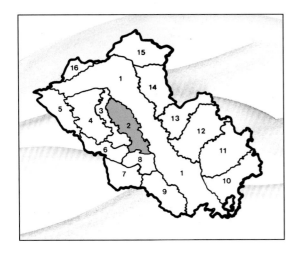

Landscape Character

In west Fermanagh the Sillees Valley forms a distinct and well-defined lowland area some three miles across. Trending north-west to south-east the valley lies close to and parallel to Lower Lough Erne yet is visually separated from it by a ridge of Lower Limestone rising to 660 feet (200 metres) at Cullen Hill. Its western edge is a dramatic scarp of Upper Limestone, forming cliffs at Knockmore, Boho and Belmore Mountain which dominate the skyline and give points of reference to the whole valley. The lowlands are choked with steep-sided drumlin hills, which are packed tighter and rise higher as one moves towards Cullen Hill. The drumlins fade away into the Arney lowlands south of Letterbreen and Bellanaleck.

The Sillees River winds slowly back and forth around and between the hills, through Carran and Ross Loughs and eventually reaches Upper Lough Erne just south of Enniskillen. It is joined by two major tributaries, the Screenagh and Boho Rivers and many smaller ones, all part of the intricate interdrumlin drainage network. Ross Lough and Carran Lough, situated below the limestone escarpment at Boho, are significant landscape features but Coolyermer Lough is almost hidden amongst drumlins in the south of the valley.

Derrygonnelly

...The village, of just over five hundred souls, is situated in drumlin country about three miles south of Lower Lough Erne and is surrounded by green hills, heathy mountains, bogs and rocky pastures. Little lakes pepper the countryside, many of them containing crannogs, those mysterious little islands made by the lake dwellers of long ago. Streams of pure spring water feed these little lakes and then larger streams flow out either into Lough Erne or into the main river of the area known as the Sillees....

William Parke 1988 [7]

Ross Lough

The drumlin hills are very striking whether viewed from within or from above. Their height, steep slopes, and sheer mass create an enclosed scene which is emphasised by small fields, tall hedges, and abundant trees. Gaps between drumlins reveal views over open, flat, ill-drained areas towards higher hills beyond. In the high-level view from Knockmore, rounded, flowing drumlins, interrupted by the few loughs, stretch away towards higher hills such as Cullen, and then disappear into the distance across Lough Erne and towards Enniskillen.

Soil drainage is best on the slopes east of Derrygonnelly and around Oakfield and Battery Hill in the south but in other parts of the valley impeded drainage is a severe agricultural handicap. Cold, heavy, structureless, gley soils encourage rush infestation, and on some of the hills farm units remain subdivided into incredibly small fields, often presenting an air of despair. However progressive farmers have enlarged fields and, with field drainage, have been able to produce good grassland for silage or grazing.

Close to the main rivers and drainage channels land is subject to seasonal flooding and some of these areas

Cowslip

are still managed as hay meadows or used for seasonal-rough grazing. This low intensity of farming supports a rich variety of wild flowers.

While farming is the dominant land use, forest plantations and woods are dispersed throughout the valley and add variety of shape, texture and seasonal colour to the local scene. Small plantations, at the same scale as the individual drumlin hills, fit well into the landscape but straight boundary lines dissecting hills interrupt the natural flowing shapes of the land. Existing hedges incorporated within the plantations help maintain a variety of tree species.

Few prehistoric sites have been discovered on lowland or hills almost completely surrounded by damp lowland. However, the drier, better soils around Derrygonnelly and Monea seem to have attracted early farmers and, along with a notable group of hilltop raths in the Drumsillagh area, there is a striking line of nine raths along the top of the Cullen Hill ridge. Crannogs are found in the small loughs. One in Ross Lough is particularly obvious and, in Tullycreevy Lough, a crannog excavated last century, produced a collection of Celtic pottery, querns and other everyday items.

Crannog, Ross Lough

Topography and history is reflected in the townland-boundaries. Large individual hills with difficult access, like Drumlish, Muckenagh, and Drumscollop (or Newtown), are recognised as large townlands while on the Cullen Hill ridge smaller, irregularly-shaped townlands reflect detailed topography and greater subdivision of farmland.

Following the 17th century Plantation a fine castle was built at Monea, whilst Derrygonnelly and Monea became established as villages; elsewhere housing remained dispersed. Along the higher slopes of Cullen Hill settlement follows parallel road lines, but in the drumlin lowland there are individual houses or groups of houses, on hilltop or hillslope sites, centrally located within each townland. The buildings which survive include some of the traditional single and 1½ storey houses, often extended and altered over the

years. The older houses are generally associated with groups of farm buildings and with their traditional siting on upper drumlin slopes they are particularly visible in the countryside. In the south of the area there are some small estates with larger houses and small parklands. New houses are being built close to the network of county roads leaving old houses derelict or serving agricultural functions.

Monea Castle

LANDSCAPE Wide valley filled with steep-sided drumlin hills: Winding flood-plain of Sillees River: Intricate pattern of small fields, tall hedges, traditional farms, small loughs and forest plantations.

FARMING Marked variation between intensive grassland production on some farms and rush-infested pasture and rough grazing: Hay meadows a local feature: Suckler cows and store cattle with some dairy herds.

WILDLIFE Wet grasslands and several small loughs in inter-drumlin hollows: Some areas of woodland and hay meadows of nature conservation interest: Nature reserve at Ross Lough, important site for over-wintering geese.

WOODLAND AND FORESTRY Woodland limited in extent but hedgerow trees give a wooded appearance: Forestry, an alternative land use on poorly-drained soils, occurs in intermediate size blocks and has a local landscape impact.

HERITAGE Early Christian settlements well represented in the east of the area: The Plantation castle at Monea, in State Care, is one of the finest examples in Fermanagh: Many older houses of traditional character.

HOUSING AND DEVELOPMENT Derrygonnelly, Monea, Springfield and Letterbreen are local centres: Dispersed traditional housing in rural areas: Replacement dwellings a particular feature close to the Derrygonnelly and Sligo roads.

RECREATION AND TOURISM Limited access provision for fishing: Visitor facilities at Monea castle: Local services in the villages.

3 THE KNOCKMORE SCARPLAND

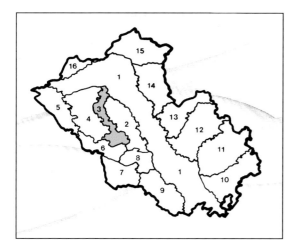

Knockmore

Landscape Character

Lying between the Sillees Valley and the extensive, bleak uplands which stretch from Lough Navar to Ballintempo is the prominent limestone escarpment which dominates skylines in west Fermanagh. Hard but soluble Upper Limestone has given rise to a strip of rugged 'karst' topography including limestone pavements, knolls, cliffs, enclosed depressions and gorges. During the last Ice Age glaciers emphasised the relief features by scouring the upper surfaces, etching crags and lake basins and leaving patches of boulder clay on the lower slopes and in valleys.

The scarp edge is most dramatic at Knockmore where 330 feet (100 metre) vertical cliffs of limestone descend into a fringe of hazel and ash woodland. Within the steeply-enclosed valleys at Boho and Kilgarro (Screenagh River) and near Correl Glen the landscape is more intimate and complicated by the admixture of small loughs, scrub woodland, patchy fields and scattered houses. The escarpment top is broken by a number of smaller scarps, chasms of tumbling streams and short horizontal steps of limestone pavements. Belmore Mountain is an outlier of the main escarpment; its massive form, capped by coniferous plantation, looms over the low ground of the Sillees and Arney valleys.

On the limestone, small streams disappear into an underground network of potholes and caves and emerge as springs and streams on the lower slopes: Noon's Hole is the deepest pothole and Reyfad pothole is part of one of the longest cave systems in Ireland. The larger rivers, the Boho and the Screenagh and part of the upper reaches of the Sillees, cut through the limestone in deep valleys with waterfalls, spectacular gorges and caves.

Towards the northern end of the scarp a number of loughs, Bunnahone, Carrick, Monawilkin, Doagh, and Fadd lie close together in irregular depressions along the broken scarp edge. Their fringing reed beds, willow and alder woodland and occasional crannogs give them a special value in the landscape.

Monawilkin

Soils, vegetation and land use closely reflect the physical characteristics of the escarpment. On the clay covered lower slopes soils, receiving water from run-off and springs, are almost continuously damp. They have limited agricultural potential, but form wet meadows and flushes, rich in grassland flowers or overgrown with alder and willow - a colourful scene in early summer.

On the steeper hill slopes soils tend to be thin and unstable and native woodland has survived in many places. Hazel dominates, along with ash, hawthorn, alder and birch. These trees create a striking landscape element in combination with the often bare, light grey, overhanging cliffs of limestone. The early season woodland plants - bluebell, wood anemone, wild garlic and primrose - are among the wide range of flora which give ground-cover under the trees. In many places, heavy grazing of livestock has reduced the diversity of the flora and restricted woodland regeneration. Some areas of scrub have been cleared.

On the upper slopes, limestone plateau and knolls, soil cover is usually thin and grass grows short with a diverse flora of lime-loving plants. The floral variety of this area is unique in Northern Ireland and, in addition

Limestone pavement

to its rare species of plants and butterflies, the limestone grassland is striking in contrast to the wet meadows, rushy fields and improved grassland elsewhere in Fermanagh. Where sandstone outcrops above the limestone there is an immediate change to acid grassland and heath with birch and oak scrub or blanket bog.

Field boundaries vary markedly within the area. On lower slopes there are overgrown hedges and ditches which contrast markedly with the drystone walls of the limestone areas. Many of the walls and hedges are not maintained as stock-proof boundaries and dereliction is often evident. Earth banks are more common on higher ground.

Coniferous forestry is virtually absent from the limestone scarpland. While planted areas come close to the broken scarp edge in the north of the area it is only

on the slopes of Belmore Mountain that coniferous plantations make a significant landscape impact.

The limestone, with its light, easily-cultivated soils and ready supply of building stone, appears to have been greatly favoured by early farmers in Fermanagh. Many Neolithic and Bronze Age stone monuments survive on prominent sites around the edge of the scarp. Particularly notable are the cup-and-ring marked stones near Boho. Raths, cashels and crannogs dating back to

Carved Cross-Shaft, Boho

Early Christian times are concentrated in the Boho valley and in the broken scarpland of the Carrick Lough area. An important Early Christian carved cross-shaft survives at Boho, and a plain shaft at Aghanaglack. Tradition and folklore are very strong in the area and there are hair-raising stories associated with many of the spectacular potholes, caves and historic sites.

In more recent times, churches and schools have been built, with Boho village becoming the meeting-place for the area. The road at the foot of the scarp is the main link within the area and from it there are connections up the Boho Valley to Belcoo and across the uplands to Garrison. Apart from these roads there is a network of tortuous farm roads and tracks up the scarp face giving farming access to many remote localities.

Housing is both dispersed and grouped, with loose settlement clusters alongside roads and in sheltered locations along the broken scarp. Many of the more remote houses are derelict, some being used for agricultural purposes. The houses are generally 1 or 1/2 storey and, with their secluded siting, small scale and associated trees, they integrate well into the surrounding landscapes. However, in the open landscape, new development can make a marked impact and some larger new bungalows on exposed sites are less in keeping with local character.

Lenaghan

Conservation Interest and Issues

LANDSCAPE The dramatic landscape of the scarp with its gorges, potholes, caves, crags, limestone pavements, woodlands and loughs is outstanding and unique in Northern Ireland.

FARMING The limestone soils are well-drained and productive: Rough grazing, small improved fields and hay meadows: Suckler cows, store cattle and sheep: Agricultural improvement: Difficult access.

WILDLIFE Limestone pavements and species-rich grasslands, native woodlands and loughs of special botanical interest.

WOODLAND AND FORESTRY Scarp woodlands a characteristic feature: Coniferous plantations on Belmore Mountain make a significant landscape impact.

HERITAGE An important concentration of archaeological sites representing most periods of Fermanagh's past up to, and including, 19th century subsistence farming.

HOUSING AND DEVELOPMENT Many older traditional houses are in a poor condition: Some of the few replacement dwellings tend to be large in scale and prominently sited.

MINERAL WORKINGS Small, disused limestone quarries.

RECREATION AND TOURISM No formal recreation facilities: Potholing and caving of growing popularity: Some of the best walking country in Fermanagh but no footpaths promoted: Excellent opportunities for educational uses and outdoor pursuits.

4 THE LOUGH NAVAR AND BALLINTEMPO UPLANDS

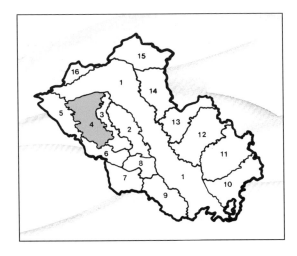

Landscape Character

The uplands of west Fermanagh stretch in a wide belt some ten miles long from the Cliffs of Magho, overlooking Lough Erne in the north, to Ora More Mountain overlooking Lough Macnean in the south. These bleak hills have been carved out of a broken and undulating sandstone plateau. Different layers of coarse grits, shales and limestones form sharp-edged escarpments, small lough basins, rock ridges and the remarkable rock pinnacles of Big Dog and Little Dog. Limestone rocks outcrop as steep, cliffed escarpments to the north, east and south of the area but to the west the land slopes gradually, the rugged sandstone crags replaced by the long rounded ridges and narrow valleys of the lowlands around Garrison.

While drainage to the west is by gentle streams, in the east the Sillees and Screenagh Rivers drain from the escarpment by deep glens. Correl Glen is one of the most spectacular glens, its steep sides and natural oak and birch woodland overhanging the boulder-strewn channel of the Sillees River.

The uplands generally lie between 500 and 1,150 feet (150 and 350 metres), and the open, uneven surface is

Correl Glen

exposed to the full force of Atlantic storms running up through Donegal Bay. In the past, ice stripped away much of the soil and, in more recent times with high rainfall and poor drainage on the shallow slopes, conditions have favoured the development of the blanket bog which now covers much of the area.

On the bog there is almost another blanket of forest, a large proportion, over half of the uplands, having been planted progressively over the last thirty years. Coniferous plantations dominate the landscape in regular blocks of uniform age. Where the terrain is

—50—

broken by rock outcrops and small loughs, the trees create a varied landscape in which swathes of conifers are interrupted by rocky, heather-clad knolls, patches of native trees -willow, birch and rowan - and loughs fringed by marsh and fen. On lower ground forestry surrounds and encloses working farms, providing a degree of shelter and contrast. However, much of the forest acts like a blanket obscuring pre-existing variations in natural vegetation and topography and in cultural features such as old farms, fields and ancient monuments.

Unplanted areas within and around the forests are crucial to the appreciation of the landscape and are important for wildlife. Open spaces include turbary plots allocated for peat cutting, nature reserves managed for particular wildlife and hilltops unsuitable for trees but now popular as viewing points. Rare plant communities, restricted to the northern Atlantic fringes of Ireland, survive on rock outcrops and in the fens, bogs, lake margins and patches of native woodland. Hen harriers benefit from the thick growth of heather and grasses which accompany the early stages of forestry. A few snipe and curlew breed in the remaining areas of bog but other upland wader birds, golden plover and dunlin, are absent.

Forestry continues to expand but the preferred sites are now at lower altitudes in the enclosed farmland to the west. Recently greater care has been taken to ensure that forestry fits into the landscape. Stream lines have been kept clear of conifers to protect water quality and broad-leaved trees have been planted to create more natural landscape features.

The uplands are distinguished by a concentration of Neolithic megaliths: standing stones, cairns, passage and court tombs. They are often sited in prominent positions around the fringe of the area on hills commanding extensive views as at Big Dog, Killy Beg and Aghanaglack. Other sites may remain undiscovered below the blanket bogs. The absence of raths and crannogs suggests the area was considered inhospitable in historic times. More recent are a number of sweat houses, located near to supplies of turf, which according to local custom were used for the treatment of rheumatism.

Dual court tomb, Aghanaglack

During the 19th century a significant farming population occupied sheltered valleys and patches of better soils. Although many sites are now lost within the forest, there remain bare earth banks and occasional lines of thorn bushes, poignant reminders of a rural community that has largely disappeared. A few farms continue to be worked, providing a tenuous thread with the past, and there are one or two groups of forestry houses. Overall the uplands are now empty and many miles can be trod along forest roads without meeting a soul.

Lough Navar

LANDSCAPE Broken plateau with heath and knolls, small loughs and deep valleys: A special wilderness appeal: Forestry plantations a dominant feature: Panoramic views of surrounding lowlands.

FARMING A few hill farms are worked; Small areas of improved grassland: Extensive rough grazing provides welcome open spaces within the forests.

WILDLIFE Rock outcrops, intact blanket bogs, small loughs and wooded valleys of special botanical interest: Moorland birds and birds of prey a feature of the unafforested areas: Five nature reserves - Correl Glen, Lough Naman Bog, Conagher, Carricknagower and Bolusty Beg: Forestry and peat-cutting reduce the special wildlife interest of the uplands.

WOODLAND AND FORESTRY Forestry, the major land-use often dominates the landscape: Small areas of semi-natural woodland and scrub on rocky scarps and in valleys.

HERITAGE Neolithic monuments a particular feature of the rocky plateau: Aghanaglack Dual Court Tomb is in State Care.

HOUSING AND DEVELOPMENT A few working farms and forestry houses. Derelict and ruined farm-houses: Radio mast at Lough Navar Forest.

MINERAL WORKINGS Widespread turbary on blanket bog.

RECREATION AND TOURISM Forest Service provides a range of recreational facilities - picnic areas, viewpoints, footpaths and nature trails: The Ulster Way includes some spectacular sections within forests at Big Dog, Conagher and Lough Navar: Several loughs stocked for fishing.

.... a wild romantic mountainous heathy district,....vast ridges of impending cliffs and precipices, stretching east and west in parallel lines, form bold and conspicuous features on the very summit of the mountains....

O.S. Memoirs 1834 [8]

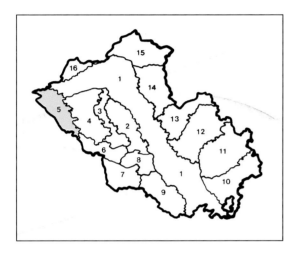

Landscape Character

Lough Melvin and the Garrison lowlands make up a secluded area of west Fermanagh close to Donegal Bay. The lowlands are edged on the south by Lough Melvin and the County River, and on the north by the River Erne. In the west they extend across the Border towards the coast at Bundoran. To the east the land rises and the lowlands gradually merge with the rugged sandstone uplands around Lough Navar, Big Dog and Ballintempo.

In the lowlands the relief is dominated by long, rounded ridges of glacial deposits, the ridges becoming shallower and the intervening valleys wider and flatter from east to west. Small rivers - the Glen, Roogagh and Bradoge - make their way west, passing between the ridges, through narrow wooded gorges and small circular lakes and crossing wide expanses of bog and wet meadows to reach Lough Melvin or eventually the coast.

Throughout the lowlands, soils are generally poorly drained and on some ridges soils are thin enough to expose sandstone boulders at the ground surface. In the past farmers reclaimed this land by removing the stones and using them to make earth banks around fields. At present, with the majority of the area

Glen Bridge

enclosed, the land is predominantly in permanent grassland. Due to the generally low intensity of agricultural use, coupled with traditional farming methods, herb-rich hay meadows are still common, some being among the best examples in Northern Ireland.

Although a few farmers have improved their land by drainage there is evidence of a widespread, gradual decline in farming activity; leading in some places to eventual dereliction. Some small units appear to have been almost abandoned but other larger units are being managed extensively for rough grazing.

Field boundaries on the lower ground are usually hedge banks with low trees, thorn bushes and shrubs. Few hedges are trimmed and invariably supplementary post and wire fences are used if stockproofing is required. On higher ground earth banks are often bare or picked out by scattered thorn bushes, but in recent years there has been a practice of planting surplus forestry trees along field boundaries to provide conifer hedges and shelter belts.

Native tree cover is low and scattered, with small clumps of broad-leaved trees providing shelter around farms or in strips along streams and river valleys. Only in the more sheltered valley locations around Garrison, Cornadarum, Roogagh Bridge and Frevagh do ash, sycamore or beech grow to any substantial height.

Unlike the Lough Navar and Ballintempo Uplands, plantations of coniferous trees on the lowlands are of a more modest scale and have lesser landscape impact because of their dispersed locations. At Drumnasreane, Muckenagh, Derrynameeo, Gorteen and Corgary only a few farms have been bought and planted as a block and forestry on this scale generally fits more comfortably into the undulating landscape.

Lough Melvin and the County River act as a physical as well as a political boundary as they divide the low undulating land around Garrison and Belcoo from the stepped gritstone hills of Leitrim and Sligo to the south. The north and south shores of Lough Melvin are quite different. The south shore dominates the scene from the north with distinct 'ladder farms' on the pronounced slopes up to the Sheenun ridge. In contrast, the north shores are low-lying and exposed with coarse boulder and shingle beaches fringed by a wind-trimmed thicket of alder and hazel. Lines of low ridges project into the lough forming points and islands, Bilberry Island, Gorminish, Rossmore Point and Rosskit Island. Reed beds flourish behind the islands and in sheltered inlets.

Lough Melvin

The lough is renowned internationally for its trout fishing, with fish caught on the light mayfly hatch which, unlike many other loughs, stretches over quite a long season. Lough Melvin's fame is partially due to the unique range in varieties of brown trout - common brown trout, ferox, gillaroo and sonaghan. Unlike some other waterways in Ireland the lough has not suffered from pollution, over-exploitation or the introduction of predators such as pike. It is probably the last lough in Europe in which all three species can be found together and it contains Arctic char which is an indication of the very clean water. The lough is also one of the few places in Northern Ireland where spring salmon can still be caught.

There is little surviving evidence of human activity in the area before the Early Christian period and it is likely that the land was thickly forested. However, numerous raths survive to the present day. Generally they were located in prominent positions along low ridges and valley sides and many have well-preserved ditches and banks, for example at Corry, Moneendogue and Leglehid. The cashel at Frevagh is more unusual and there is also a stone cross and well marking an early church site known as Kilcoo.

Today's settlement pattern is one of small, dispersed farms and houses strung along roads or forming widely-spaced clusters around crossroads and bridges - Scribbagh, Kilcoo, Roogagh Bridge, Glen Bridge and Farrancassidy. Formerly houses were even more widely distributed and the ruins of many derelict sites, located well away from any county road, are now marked by small groups of trees.

The traditional houses in the countryside were small single or 1½ storey houses. Although many are still occupied, unless modernised they provide a standard of accommodation below that now normally expected. A few thatched farmhouses survive. As in other parts of Fermanagh there is a noticeable relocation of settlement towards the main roads and especially road junctions, so that new bungalows and houses of very mixed architectural styles make a considerable impact along the roads out of Garrison and Belleek.

Garrison is the only village in the area and it has both a strategic and picturesque situation at the head of Lough Melvin. It has long been a centre for fishing and the village is developing its recreational role with an outdoor pursuits centre and holiday accommodation.

Species-rich hay meadow

Hedge with Dog Rose

LANDSCAPE Long, rounded glacial ridges with intervening valleys and bogs: Some medium-sized forestry blocks: Traditional farm buildings within patchwork of small fields.

FARMING Traditional farm practices and farm landscapes: Hay meadows, rush-infested pasture and overgrown hedges: Suckler herds on small farms: General decline in agricultural activity.

WILDLIFE Botanically rich hay meadows, amongst the best examples in Northern Ireland: Areas of bog and wet grassland, important for snipe and curlew: Lough Melvin reed beds and shoreline woodland: Rare trout varieties and char in Lough Melvin.

WOODLAND AND FORESTRY Natural woodland around the shores and islands of Lough Melvin and in the river valleys: Mixed trees accompany most older dwellings: Expansion of coniferous forestry in enclosed farmland.

HERITAGE Good examples of raths: Selection of Listed vernacular farmhouses.

HOUSING AND DEVELOPMENT Dispersed, small traditional farmhouses: Often sub-standard accommodation: High levels of dereliction: New housing concentrated close to main roads and at junctions.

MINERAL WORKING Widespread turbary on lowland bogs.

RECREATION AND TOURISM Outdoor pursuits, water sports and fishing at Lough Melvin: Guest-house accommodation and local services at Garrison.

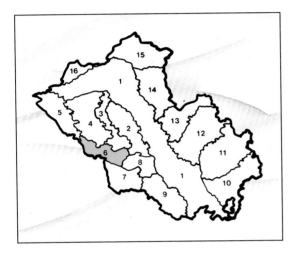

Landscape Character

The Lough Macnean valley is in the south-west of Fermanagh bordering County Leitrim. Lying on a north-west to south-east axis the valley has two loughs, Upper and Lower Lough Macnean, which stretch some eight or nine miles in length but generally are little more than one mile wide. The valley was formed by glaciers moving from east to west, excavating deep basins in softer rocks and scouring harder rocks to create impressive steep valley sides and prominent rocky scarps, notably at Hanging Rock and Drumelly Rocks. To the east the valley opens out to the flat Arney valley, while to the north-west it connects with the Garrison lowlands.

Carboniferous limestones, sandstones and shales underlie the area and their varied outcrops contribute to the character of the valley sides. To the north, hard Upper Limestone outcrops along the slopes of Belmore Mountain in an impressive craggy escarpment broken by solution hollows, rock steps, knolls and small valleys. The larger Lurgan valley, which separates Belmore Mountain from the uplands to the west, cuts through sandstone and limestone with waterfalls marking the harder rock strata.

Limestone underlies the low-lying strip of land which separates the two loughs at Belcoo and connects the limestone crags of Belmore Mountain with the remarkable Marlbank escarpment to the south. Rocky knolls of limestone protrude through the boulder clay covering the valley bottom around Holywell and Aughrim.

Further west and around much of Upper Lough Macnean beds of sandstone, grits and shales form the long slopes broken by small outcrops of rock running up towards Ora More and Ballintempo in the north and the prominent Thur Mountain in County Leitrim.

Lower Lough Macnean

Lurgan Valley

The loughs contrast in character. Around the larger, Upper Lough, the shoreline is broken by wooded promontories between and behind which lie sheltered bays with fringing reed swamps. A number of islands such as Kilrooscagh, Rosscorkey and Inishteen, interrupt the expanse of water and shorelines have a natural succession of swamp, fen and carr woodland. The poorer soils and rocky hillsides, as at Drumelly Rocks, are not farmed intensively, fields tend to be rush-infested, hedges are overgrown and there is some scrub encroachment.

Church at Upper Lough Macnean

Lower Lough Macnean is more confined by its steep surrounding limestone scarpland; the drama of the hills, in particular Hanging Rock, making a major contribution to its outstanding landscape setting. Although the lough has a more developed and agricultural shoreline, there are open, wet, grasslands at Cushrush Island contrasting with thick woodland at Corry Point. Soils over the limestone rock produce good-quality grassland and the southern shores and the lower slopes around the Cladagh River are farmed intensively. North of the loughs, between Templenaffrin and Drumharriff, farm units are smaller but there is also intensive cattle and sheep grazing.

Woods and scrub form an incomplete band around the steeper limestone slopes of Belmore Mountain and the Lurgan valley. Damp, rushy meadow and flushes occur at the spring-line and above it there is limestone grassland of special botanical interest. Scrub clearance and application of fertilizers have reduced the value of these habitats for wildlife.

The valley has some significant archaeological sites. At Cushrush Island evidence has been found of Mesolithic people fishing, gathering and hunting some 9,000 years ago. With the introduction of farming the light limestone soils were favoured for settlement

sites and surviving from that time are stone burial monuments, for example the court tomb at Carrickmacsparrow. Later farming and settlement moved lower down the slopes as indicated today by numerous raths and several crannogs in the loughs. The merging of Christian and pagan cultures is suggested by the association of the church at Holywell with an important natural spring. Ruined medieval churches survive at Holywell and Templenaffrin, their graveyards still in use.

Townland boundaries vary with the topography of the area; long narrow townlands, divided into 'ladder farms', run up higher slopes but on lower land very irregular townlands encircle the drumlin hills. Thus, on the slopes of Belmore Mountain, farmhouses are located on steps within each strip, the houses at upper levels now mostly derelict. In contrast, close to the Arney River, in Corrateskin and Derreens West, the small farms with gardens make a loose cluster on the low hill, which forms the centre of each townland.

Gardenhill estate, north of Belcoo, has its origins in the Plantation period, its 17th century house set in a small-scale parkland landscape with broad-leaf and coniferous woods contrasting with the surrounding farmed hill slopes.

Belcoo, the only village in the area, has an attractive setting between the loughs. New housing is located around the village and there is open space running down to the shore of Lower Lough Macnean.

Conservation Interest and Issues

LANDSCAPE The combination of the dramatic limestone crags and the loughs with their surrounding natural vegetation and farmland is outstanding in Northern Ireland.

FARMING Varies from intensively-farmed, improved grasslands around Lower Lough Macnean and on the slopes of Belmore Mountain to small holdings with low intensity grazing around Upper Lough Macnean: Sheep, suckler cows and store cattle.

WILDLIFE Species-rich grassland on limestone. Areas of semi-natural woodland and scrub: Reed swamps and fen on the lough shores: Corry Point Wood is a nature reserve: One of Northern Ireland's few flocks of Greenland white fronted geese spend the winter on the lough.

WOODLAND AND FORESTRY Semi-natural hillside and lough-shore woodland and scrub: Linear hillside plantations.

HERITAGE Wide range of archaeological sites including an important group of Early Christian monuments: Two medieval churches: Interesting vernacular farm buildings.

HOUSING AND DEVELOPMENT Smaller old dwellings are being replaced by modern houses: Some ribbon development overlooking Lower Lough Macnean.

MINERAL WORKINGS Quarrying for roadstone and magnesia limestone at Kiltyfelan is a feature of the highly visible hillside of Belmore Mountain.

RECREATION AND TOURISM Opportunities for low-key water-borne activities and fishing: Outdoor Education Centre at Gortatole: Ulster Way crosses the valley.

Holywell

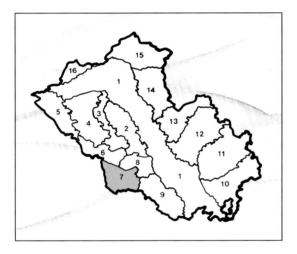

Landscape Character

The south-west corner of Fermanagh extends to the summit of Cuilcagh, which at 2,195 feet (665m) is the only true mountain in Fermanagh. Cuilcagh and the Marlbank provide some of the most dramatic country-side in the county.

The area is distinguished by its underlying Carboniferous strata dipping slightly to the south and west. Upper Limestone forms a magnificent escarpment around the upland from the Marlbank and Hanging Rock through Florence Court to Benaughlin and Greenan Rock. The hard, soluble limestone is riddled with potholes and caves forming classic karst features of limestone pavements, gorges and dry valleys. On the Marlbank prominent rounded hills, known as reef knolls, rise above the general land surface, for example at Crossmurrin, Legnabrocky and Gortmaconnell.

Marlbank

Overlying the limestones are impermeable flagstones and shales which form the long broken slopes of Cuilcagh Mountain. Many streams drain the slopes and then plunge underground near the junction of the limestone to become part of the most extensive cave system in Ireland. The summit of Cuilcagh is capped by coarse sandstone forming a gritstone edge more typical of the Leitrim Hills to the south and reminiscent of the peaks of the Yorkshire Dales in England.

In the last Ice Age, ice flow from the east was split into two streams by the Cuilcagh upland. One stream moved through the Lower Macnean Valley and the other south through the Swanlinbar gap, the ice movement trimming the edges of the limestone to form sharp cliffs at Hanging Rock and Benaughlin. Boulder clay was spread in rounded hills at the base of the escarpment around Florence Court and Doohatty Glebe and in patches on the upper slopes of the Marlbank.

The geology and its associated drainage and soils is also responsible for great contrasts in the natural vegetation cover. Ranging from montane grassland on the summit it proceeds downhill through blanket bog, limestone grassland, gorge and scarp woodlands to wet meadows at the base of the Marlbank.

Blanket Bog, Cuilcagh

On the limestone plateau vegetation differs greatly between the thin light soils on limestone pavements, peats in poorly drained hollows and gley soils on the thicker boulder clays. The thin limestone soils are characterised by a herb-rich grassland, and ferns and mosses are found in fissures or grykes within the pavements. On steeper slopes, where grazing has been less intensive, low hazel scrub grows in irregular patches. The sink-holes and steep gorges have a more luxuriant woodland cover and under the trees there is a carpet of woodland flowers. On the patches of wetter gley soils there is often a fen meadow with unusual mixtures of iris, rushes, bog myrtle and orchid. However agricultural improvements on the Marlbank have involved clearance of hazel scrub, drainage of wet meadows and application of fertilizer to limestone grasslands. Collectively this activity has reduced the

extent and diversity of wildlife habitats.

The peat covered slopes of Cuilcagh are dominated by heather with cotton grasses in the damper areas and rushes and sedges on the lower slopes. Large areas of blanket bog, traditionally cut by hand, are now being cut mechanically. The summit, and its three miles of gritstone cliffs, is one of the most remote locations in Northern Ireland. The altitude and exposure, combined with the geographical isolation, have ensured the survival of several rare plants; creeping willow, cowberry and starry-saxifrage.

Throughout this area, field enclosures have been constrained by the distribution of thicker soils and limestone pavements. Today's fields tend to be large and irregular but remains of older, possibly prehistoric, fields are smaller, enclosing the better land around farmsteads. Burial monuments of the Neolithic and Bronze Ages are found across the area. These include several megalithic tombs, notably Clyhannagh dual court tomb, and prominent cairns on Cuilcagh and Benaughlin. The oldest farm sites identified, date back to the Early Christian period, in the form of cashels and raths. Over thirty such sites have been discovered.

There are ruins of a 17th century church at Killesher.

Cashel, Cullentragh

A further element of diversity in the landscape is introduced by Florence Court house and estate. The house itself is dramatically sited below the limestone scarp, with views across the lawns to the Arney valley. The gardens and enclosing woodlands create an atmosphere of elegance and comfort which contrasts with the harsh rock outcrops and scrub woodlands of overlooking Benaughlin - a masterpiece of 18th century landscaping. Much of the former estate and deer park is now given over to forestry, including forest park recreation facilities. Forestry occupies several other prominent sites along the limestone escarpment.

Today the area is sparsely populated with a number of farms on the Marlbank and around the foot of the escarpment. A much larger rural community once occupied the limestone plateau but many of the houses are now derelict. Some new bungalows have replaced the small traditional houses. Larger farmhouses are more characteristic of the lower slopes and many of these $1\frac{1}{2}$ or 2 storey houses have been maintained and improved.

The dramatic scenery, caves and botanical interest have attracted visitors to the area for many years. It is only relatively recently that the development of facilities at Marble Arch Cave and Florence Court has drawn larger crowds to these particular attractions but the countryside around remains remarkably quiet.

Marble Arch Cave   Photo : NITB

Conservation Interest and Issues

LANDSCAPE The limestone landforms, the marked contrast between rock types and the associated patterns of natural vegetation and land use are remarkable and unique in Northern Ireland.

FARMING Extensive rough grazing on mountain and limestone: Few improved fields: Sheep and beef cattle.

WILDLIFE A concentration of botanical interest including, limestone grassland and pavements, natural woodlands, blanket bog and montane grassland, exceptional in Northern Ireland: Nature reserves at Crossmurrin, Hanging Rock, Marble Arch, Killesher, Florence Court and Doohatty Glebe.

WOODLAND AND FORESTRY Semi-natural gorge and scarp woodlands: Forest plantations on the escarpment at Florence Court and Doohatty Glebe: Planting and management of broad-leaf woodland at Florence Court.

HERITAGE Good cross-section of archaeological sites including megalithic tombs at Clyhannagh and Greenan,

....Marble Arch cave near Enniskillen is a living river cave, with a dramatic descent from the surface to the Claddagh river, an enchanting boat ride up dark waters and a stroll up a passage "decorated" with stalactites and stalagmites. With fine rock structure, sparkling waters and exquisite stalactite formations this must be the most beautiful cave for the casual visitor to admire...
Gareth Jones 1987 [9]

cairns on Cuilcagh and Benaughlin and many Early Christian cashels and raths: Some field boundaries may be of prehistoric origin: Florence Court house, gardens and restored mill.

HOUSING AND DEVELOPMENT The area is sparsely populated: Houses tend to be small and associated with farms: Buildings prominent in open landscape.

MINERAL WORKING Disused limestone quarries at Gortalughany: Extensive peat cutting on slopes of Cuilcagh.

RECREATION AND TOURISM Marble Arch caves a popular tourist attraction in association with Florence Court and the Marlbank scenic loop: Attractive and well-used section of the Ulster Way including the Cladagh valley and the challenging ascent of Cuilcagh: Good viewpoint at Gortalughany: Informal recreation facilities in the Florence Court Forest Park and National Trust estate: Exploratory caving and rock climbing.

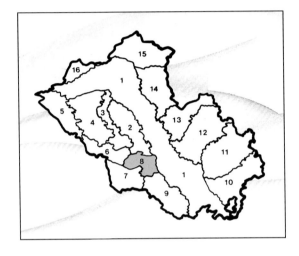

Landscape Character

Between the uplands of west Fermanagh, Belmore and the Cuilcagh Mountains, is the wide valley of the Arney River, a river which drains Lower Lough Macnean and the uplands and flows east to join Upper Lough Erne. Strictly speaking it is not a valley but a broad, flat, glacial trough through which the river now meanders uncertainly to the lakeland heart of Fermanagh. To the north lie the tall, steep-sided drumlins of the Sillees Valley and to the east the inundated wetlands of Upper Lough Erne.

Unlike much of the rest of lowland Fermanagh the valley floor is distinguished by wide, flat spaces between low hills. Much of this lowland, lying at between 160-200 feet (50-60 metres) has damp peaty soils, generally farmed, but partly covered with scrub woodland and surviving cut-over and raised bogs. The best remaining bogs at Clontymullan, Tattenamona and Lisblake support some rare species of sedge and are important for snipe and curlew.

The shallow hills which rise out of the flat lowland make islands of small rushy fields and hay meadows surrounded by thick overgrown hedges. This small

Curlew   *photo : Ron Thompson*

The Arney Lowlands

....Here unity is not determined by physical form. The community exists on its straggle of damp hills in a perpetual state of negotiation. It shifts and reshapes as people meet, joining for work and gathering at night in ceilis....

Henry Glassie 1982 [10]

scale mosaic provides the ideal habitat for corncrakes which nest in the long grass of hay fields. Their numbers have fallen sharply all over Northern Ireland and this part of Fermanagh appears to be one of the few remaining areas to which a few birds return each spring.

For a long period of human history the lowland had a thick covering of oak, elm, ash and alder and, with poor access, was not favoured for early settlement. A few raths, located on the higher drumlin hills, are found on the edges of the area.

It was the improved agricultural techniques and new roads of the 18th century which opened up this land and resulted, over the following century, in a division into numerous farms. Each hill, usually a separate townland, accommodates a dispersed group of small farmhouses, linked by the straight roads which bump along from one hill to the next. Communities are small and each hill, townland, road and crossroads is a place in itself. The bordering limestone escarpments peer over the horizon, each with a distinctive profile.

Viewed from these escarpments the wide valley appears as a dense mosaic of mottled greens and drab browns

speckled with the brilliant whites of houses. The small fields with tall hedges give the impression of a wooded countryside but the pattern is interrupted by groups of enlarged and improved fields and dull patches of bog. The line of the disused railway from Enniskillen to Sligo has, in part, been incorporated in the road network, its associated buildings now converted as dwellings.

Restored Railway Cottage

Arney and Macken are the settlements in the area, but they are tiny. Most settlement is concentrated at crossroads or dispersed as ribbon development close to the road network of the area. The older, small traditional houses sometimes provide sub-standard accommodation. The more remote sites are derelict with replacement dwellings favouring roadside locations.

Conservation Interest and Issues

LANDSCAPE Broad, flat, glacial trough between the hills of west Fermanagh: Farms with small fields are grouped on low hills standing above surrounding damp lowland and bog.

FARMING Varied pattern of farm holdings: Intensive grassland on large, improved fields: Rough grazing on small, rush-infested fields and bog margins: Hay meadows, suckler herds and some dairying.

WILDLIFE Important raised bogs at Clontymullan, Tattenamona and Lisblake: Corncrakes favour the mixed habitats of bog, rushy fields, hay meadows and improved grassland.

WOODLAND AND FORESTRY Small, mixed woods around farmhouses and birch and willow scrub on cut-over bogs: Small coniferous plantation at Corraglass.

HERITAGE Archaeological sites limited to some raths on the higher land.

HOUSING AND DEVELOPMENT Scattered traditional farmhouses: New replacement dwellings with roadside locations.

RECREATION AND TOURISM Access for fishing to the Arney River: A number of farm guest-houses: Local services.

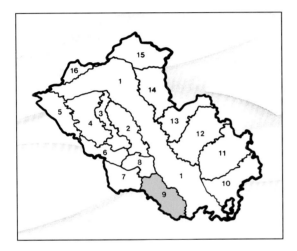

Landscape Character

The Slieve Russel range is a small, isolated upland block which forms the southern boundary of Fermanagh. The flat-topped range rising to 1,322 feet (403m) has steep slopes on all sides dissected by small glens which run down into complex glacial deposits on the lower slopes. To the east the area includes the lowlands around Derrylin. To the north there is the Swanlinbar River and the lowlands around Kinawley.

Geologically the hills are similar to the adjacent Cuilcagh Mountain with a succession of limestones, shales and sandstones - from bottom to top - the Upper Limestone outcropping in a ring around the lower and middle slopes.

Despite the geological similarity the uplands do not have the dramatic relief associated with the limestones further west and north. However, limestone knolls are a notable feature on the northern slopes from Springtown Rock to Carn Hill. The eastern slopes are quarried for limestone at Gortmullan. The two major summits, Slieve Russel in the south and Molly Mountain, at the northern apex of the uplands, are almost separated by the steep-sided glens of the Owengar River, a tributary of the Cladagh or Swanlinbar River.

Although the uplands were completely over-ridden by ice during the last Ice Age the ice flow was channelled to either side leaving roughly aligned drumlin topography on the lower slopes, with an area of glacial gravel deposits along the Derrylin to Ballyconnell Road. Further east, a wide expanse of lowland bog intervenes, lying between and around small hills of boulder clay, before the drumlin hills grow taller and more crowded towards the shores of Upper Lough Erne.

Tiravree Glebe and Gortacarn

In the glacial channel or trough to the north of the upland block the Cladagh or Swanlinbar River wriggles its way through damp lowland with low elongated hills of varying extent.

This is a complex landscape unit with contrasting elements of upland and lowland but it is bound together by the dominance of Slieve Russel.

The summit area of the mountain has a cover of blanket bog disturbed by turf cutting and erosion. There, and on the upper slopes, heath is often replaced by rush-infested rough grazing which in places, particularly around Molly Mountain, has been improved. Ladder farms are striking features of the hillsides, the land divided by banks with scattered gorse and thorn bushes. The steeper middle slopes, especially on the limestone, retain fragments of scrub woodland dominated by hazel and ash. These woodlands blend into the larger coniferous plantation of Derrylin Wood at Mullynaherb.

On the lower slopes, and on the lowlands to the east and north of the uplands, there is a mosaic of small fields, some rushy and with overgrown hedges, some hay meadows, and others farmed intensively for grassland production. The intervening bogs have experienced widespread modification through drainage, reclamation and turbary. Moninea bog, near Teemore Cross, is an outstanding example of an intact lowland raised bog, though marginally affected by peat cutting. Some older cut-over bogs have been colonised by birch and willow scrub. Again there is a marked contrast between recently improved fields, rush-infested pasture, remaining bogs and abandoned fields with scrub encroachment.

The oldest archaeological sites are Neolithic stone monuments associated with the limestone outcrop on the slopes of Molly Mountain. Several raths occur on drumlin hills on the lower slopes and there is a cashel on the limestone at Clonturkle and a crannog in Dunderg Lough. Sweat-houses, for the relief of rheumatism and other complaints, occur in Sheetrim and Drumdony townlands.

Kinawley (Cell-Naile) was an early monastery founded by St Naile. The low ridge on which the ruined medieval church stands is underlain by a block of limestone and St Naile's Well, a spring in the limestone, is known locally as a cure for warts and tumours. The ruined church at Callowhill was built in the early 17th century.

Moninea Bog

....." There's a cure in Saint Naile's Well.

" If you had any external ailments or warts or growths on your hand, if you'd rub a wee drop of the water to it, and cut the sign of the cross in the name of the Father, Son, and Holy Ghost, your wee warts or lumps or tumours or anything like that would diminish away.

" This is in Kinawley, and the water's risin....it's as clear as crystal.

" It's just boilin up there.

" And it's supposed to cure any external warts or lumps of any kind that would come on your hands.

" Saint Naile, he said he'd leave the cure behind him.

" And he put his hand down like that and he cut the sign of the cross....

Peter Flanagan 1982 [11]

Today settlement varies with the topography of the area. In the upland area farms are spread out along lanes which run up the slopes and then extend in short lengths across slight breaks in the slope. Despite isolated locations many of the farmhouses are occupied and are associated with small but modern farm buildings. Newer housing is generally concentrated on the lower slopes beside the main roads. The mixed pattern of woodland, ladder farms, varied grassland, forestry, heath and dispersed farms creates a complex and discordant scene.

On the lowlands, farm and field size is small, with groups of farms clustering on each low hill. Thatched houses are a notable feature. Derrylin is the main settlement in the area, and in its linear form it stretches for over a mile along the Enniskillen Road. Kinawley is a locally important community centre and another loose settlement cluster has developed around the church and school at Teemore Cross.

Molly Mountain

....The advantages of reclaiming are becoming so well known and appreciated that cultivation is now making rapid progress up the mountain, and the fortunate presence of marle on the Sleive Russel range of hills greatly facilitate the efforts of the farmers. In some instances fields of corn may be seen at an elevation of 800 feet above the level of the sea, and the very extremities of the little glens running nearly to the summit of the high ground are now turned to some account....

O.S.Memoirs 1834-5 [12]

Conservation Interest and Issues

LANDSCAPE Steep-sided upland rising above low drumlin hills and intervening damp lowland: Contrasting land uses of hill and lowland farm, forest and bog.

FARMING Intensification and dereliction: Traditional haymaking.

WILDLIFE Undisturbed lowland raised bogs, for example Moninea: Corncrake habitats.

WOODLAND AND FORESTRY Semi-natural woodlands on the steeper slopes and glens: Hillside coniferous forestry: Small areas of mixed woodland around large farms and houses.

HERITAGE Good range of archaeological sites from prehistoric burial monuments on Molly Mountain to an important ecclesiastical site at Kinawley; Plantation period church at Callowhill: Concentration of thatched houses.

HOUSING AND DEVELOPMENT Concentration of housing development on the lower slopes and lowland around Derrylin and Kinawley: Skyline radio mast on Molly Mountain.

MINERAL WORKING Limestone quarries, gravel pits and processing industries near the Derrylin to Ballyconnell road.

RECREATION AND TOURISM The Ulster Way crosses the area on roads: Scenic route with viewpoint on Molly Mountain: Local services at Derrylin: Work to re-open navigation on the Ballyconnell Canal and Woodford River.

10 NEWTOWNBUTLER AND ROSSLEA LOWLANDS

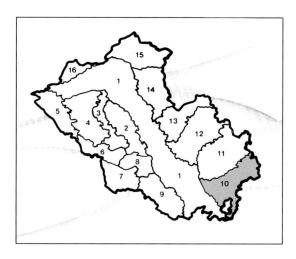

In the south-west corner of Fermanagh, between the Border which follows the Finn and Lacky Rivers and the Carnrock and Mullaghfad Hills, lies a wide belt of lowland with drumlins. The drumlin hills line up in ridges which swing across the area from east to west and it is these ridges which have influenced the pattern of rivers, lines of communication and settlement.

In the south the drumlins form low rounded hills or ridges rising above wide, wet intervening hollows. The flat, low-lying land is boggy with occasional small lakes. Open views in all directions are bounded by low drumlin hills. The River Finn at the southern edge has an extensive flood plain and is claimed to be the finest lowland river in the north of Ireland.

To the north of the Newtownbutler-Rosslea road the drumlin hills increase in height and are more tightly

Knockawaddy and Derrymeen

packed together with steep intervening valleys. Some of the steeper hills retain planted hilltop raths and, with the generally wooded character of the thorn hedges, the countryside has a well-wooded appearance.

Between Donagh and Dernawilt along the foot of the Carnrock hills the drumlin hills give way to a more pronounced valley and chain of small, spring-fed loughs. With their fringing reed swamps, carr woodlands and wet meadows the loughs are attractive landscape features and important wildlife habitats. They also contain a number of crannogs.

Mount Sedborough Lough

On the whole this drumlin belt is an uninterrupted area of pastoral farming - a land of cattle, grass, tall over-grown hedges, small farms and winding lanes. Old lime kilns and corn mills are however an indication of past arable farming; they provide local landscape interest.

Today grassland varies, a reflection of drainage and management on the wet lowland in contrast to the well-drained drumlin slopes. Farm size also varies from place to place. Along the Border, at for example Knockballymore (Lislea townland) and around Newtownbutler and Magheraveely, there are some small estates with fine houses, service buildings, lodges and tree-lined drives. Elsewhere farms are smaller with generally single storey farmhouses scattered around the sides of drumlins and reached by long lanes off the county roads. Few roads sub-divide the area around Newtownbutler, but nearer Rosslea and along the foot of the Carnrock and Mullaghfad Hills, small farms are grouped in loose clusters along the many farm lanes and short interconnecting roads.

At a few crossroads, as at Aghadrumsee, there are groups of houses with perhaps a church, post office, garage and school, but otherwise the only villages in the area are Newtownbutler and Rosslea which lie at opposite ends of the undulating lowland. Newtownbutler, a Plantation town founded on Sir Stephen Butler's lands in the early 17th century, retains a lot of character in its four main streets. Rosslea, situated at a bridging point of the River Finn, has a curved main street which, along with the woodland on the adjacent Spring Grove estate, gives a sense of enclosure unusual in Fermanagh villages. Donagh is a small settlement once associated with Donagh House, and later a school and a church.

Finn River, Ballyhoe Bridge

LANDSCAPE A broad expanse of widely-spaced drumlins with occasional small loughs and bounded by the Rivers Finn and Lacky.

FARMING Farming intensity varies considerably within the area: Intensive dairy herds and beef cattle: Some areas of declining activity.

WILDLIFE The Finn and Lacky Rivers are amongst the very few unaltered lowland watercourses in Northern Ireland: Finn floods important for wintering wildfowl: Cornagague Wood and Lough nature reserve.

WOODLAND AND FORESTRY Individual trees, parkland and tall unmanaged hedges: Small areas of semi-natural woodland on steeper drumlin slopes: No significant forestry.

HERITAGE Early Christian settlement, raths and crannogs concentrated in north of area: Number of sweat-houses; Remnants of small Plantation estates: Older vernacular houses, some with thatched roofs: Larger houses on small estates and large farms: Many 19th century farmhouses.

HOUSING AND DEVELOPMENT Traditional buildings scattered throughout the countryside: New houses often in roadside locations.

RECREATION AND TOURISM Facilities for fishing at Killyfole and Corranny Loughs: Local services at Newtownbutler and Rosslea.

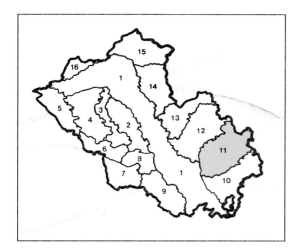

Mullaghfad Forest

Landscape Character

Situated between Fivemiletown and Rosslea, in the east of Fermanagh, is an extensive area of rolling uplands - the Carnrock and Cooneen Hills - stretching from Slieve Beagh, on the border with Tyrone and Monaghan, to the outskirts of Lisnaskea and Brookeborough.

Although less distinctive topographically, this upland block is geologically similar to those of west Fermanagh, with a prominent escarpment of Upper Limestone capped by gritstone forming the basis for the steep slopes to the south. Above the limestone, and dipping to the north and east, sandstones form the undulating hills which are deeply dissected by the Cooneen Water and the Colebrooke River valleys. On its northern limit the geological Clogher Valley Fault brings less resistant limestones and shales to the surface.

The southern edge of the uplands presents a strong line of hills with summits commanding tremendous views of the lowland plains to the south, for example at Carnrock viewpoint. Steep south-facing slopes are interrupted by small streams in steep wooded glens. Towards the north lies the broken surface of the uplands, with flat-topped hills and rounded ridges separated by deep valleys and punctuated by small round lakes. Blanket bog covers the summits but on the slopes and in the valleys boulder clay forms small drumlin hills.

Despite severe disadvantages the uplands have in the past been brought into agricultural use. Small farms and their regular patterns of fields extend from the lower valleys way up onto the higher slopes and hills: Ladder farms are notable on the south-facing escarpment. Now some of the small farms are almost derelict, and ruined houses sit at the end of overgrown green lanes amidst rushy fields and ditches. Only the summit hills and flat ridges with their thick cover of blanket bog, have avoided intensive agriculture. Instead these bogs have been valued for fuel and their bleak surfaces are etched with past cuttings and tracks.

This upland landscape has changed dramatically in the last 30 years or so. As families moved out and sold their farms, forestry has moved in with extensive conifer plantations. Because of the small size and varied locations of farms acquired, the forestry has taken on a very broken and irregular pattern. Even the largest area of forest at Mullaghfad is relieved by strips of farmland, turbary plots and small loughs. However, forestry now

Lough Corry

accounts for about two fifths of the area and is an ubiquitous feature of the landscape.

In many cases forestry contributes positively to the landscape character, adding shelter and enclosure to the desolate hills and ruined farms. Tree species are limited but it is the intermingling of broad-leaved trees around plantation edges and streams which adds to the variety in age, structure and seasonal colour, making attractive valley landscapes.

Active farming continues on the slopes around the uplands and within the valleys; but these areas present sharp contrasts. Newly-drained land with lush rye-grass can be found side by side with rush-infested land and overgrown hedges. Peat remains a source of fuel, with mechanical cutting evident in some areas.

Prehistoric and later monuments are in general located around the edges of the area. At Cooneen and Agheeghter there are groups of prehistoric monuments. Raths of the Early Christian period are located on prominent sites. The townlands are perpetuated in the names and divisions of some afforested areas.

There are no villages within the area and Cooneen crossroads, with its churches, post office, housing and old school, is the most significant community centre. It once had a corn and flax mill and a monthly fair for cattle. Elsewhere housing is dispersed on farms along the valleys and around the entire hill area, with some small groups at crossroad junctions. On the southern slopes houses are distributed along roads or lanes parallel to the slopes - a traditional settlement pattern associated with the ladder farms. Houses are generally set within small farmyards and retain traditional design features. However a few larger houses have a markedly individual design, as at Armagh Manor.

Church, Mullaghfad

LANDSCAPE Extensive area of rolling hills deeply dissected by long river valleys: Bounded by prominent escarpment on the south: Forestry.

FARMING Opposite trends of dereliction and improvement: Many small farms used for extensive grazing.

WILDLIFE Upland blanket bog and wet grassland used by snipe and curlew: Some areas of intact bog with pool and hummock complex: Small upland loughs.

WOODLAND AND FORESTRY Forestry is a major land use: Fragmented plantations with open spaces, different age groups and some broad-leaved species.

HERITAGE Prehistoric monuments at Cooneen and Agheeghter: Good examples of Early Christian raths: Holy wells as at Stranafeley: Some ruins of corn and flax mills: Millstones once made at Carnrock.

HOUSING AND DEVELOPMENT Traditional housing modest in scale but many such houses abandoned: New houses have roadside locations in vicinity of neighbouring towns - Rosslea, Lisnaskea, Brookeborough and Fivemiletown: Radio mast at Carnrock.

MINERAL WORKINGS Limestone is extracted from a quarry at Slush Hill.

RECREATION AND TOURISM Low key facilities: Small car park and viewpoint at Carnrock: Corry Lough stocked with trout for game fishing: Ulster Way traverses area through forest plantations.

12 COLEBROOKE AND TEMPO RIVER VALLEY

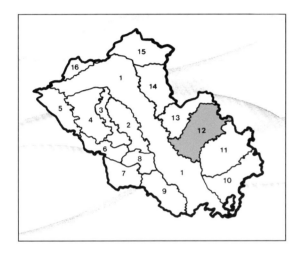

Landscape Character

Lying in the east of Fermanagh and between the two well-defined uplands, the Carnrock and Mullaghfad Hills and the Topped and Brougher Mountain Uplands, is a broad area of lowland, some five miles across. The hills give distant but clear boundaries to the lowland and create a corridor routeway, an extension of the Clogher Valley, into Fermanagh. Near Fivemiletown the county boundary follows a low, almost indistinguishable, watershed and within Fermanagh drainage is carried west to Upper Lough Erne by the Colebrooke River and its tributaries, the Tempo and Many Burns Rivers.

The lowland, while based on Carboniferous limestones and shales, is covered by boulder clay deposited in the form of small drumlin hills of varying size and height and long, low, winding ridges (eskers) of glacial sand and gravel, particularly prominent between Brookeborough and Fivemiletown. Solid rock outcrops in small areas, for example at the Crievehill limestone quarries, and at Brookeborough and Lisbellaw. Drumlin hills decrease in height west towards the Erne, but in the north and adjacent to the fault-aligned valley containing the Tempo River and Lough Eyes, there are higher hill ridges parallel to the river.

Shanco

Flat land occurs between the drumlin hills and ridges, physically linked by rivers and streams. Some flat areas are managed for hay meadows or grazing, but elsewhere persistent waterlogging has resulted in pockets of lowland bog and some small lakes. Much of the peat has been worked for turf in the past and some bogs are still being cut. Bog vegetation has been disturbed but many areas are now being colonised by birch and willow scrub. Bogs and lowland heath provide valuable habitats for wildlife in the farmed countryside.

Farming tends to be progressive, dominated by medium-sized farm businesses. Silage and, to a much lesser extent, hay is produced for winter fodder: dairying and cattle-rearing are the main farm activities. Fields are large by Fermanagh standards and hedges are variably trimmed or overgrown with notable tall, mature

Ardunshin Bridge

House at Monibbaghan

Mountain, its surface dotted with five wooded crannogs.

Housing tends to be associated with farms. Most older houses are located on the sides or tops of drumlins or ridges, with access by private farm lanes. Each townland may have two or three such houses, and at the end of green lanes there may be one or more derelict farmhouses. Most of the farm dwellings have been periodically modernized but elements of traditional design are retained in many cases. Some farmhouses are larger, often approaching the size and status of a small country house and their settings reflect those of the large country houses: a long drive with avenues of beech, a small parkland of mature trees in a field in front of the house, clipped hedges and a formal gateway.

The Tempo Manor and Colebrooke estates and a number of smaller estates, like Snowhill, have buildings with a special architectural interest; gate lodges, gates, walled gardens, houses and ornamental bridges. Distinctive buildings associated with the disused Clogher Valley Railway have been converted to dwellings as have old schools and other buildings formerly in community use.

The lowland is criss-crossed by a number of minor roads

trees. Groups of mixed trees are found around most farmhouses and trees are also a feature of hilltop raths. Raths and tree-rings are particularly evident around Brookeborough and along the Tempo River valley.

In this undulating landscape of tightly-hedged fields the Colebrooke and Tempo Manor estates make a distinct impact through their large-scale, mature trees, mixed woodland and parkland. Also, Lough Eyes, the largest lough in the area, has a dramatic landscape setting below the steep wooded hillside of Topped

and along the edges are the main roads from Enniskillen to Fivemiletown and to Fintona. Several villages and hamlets, originally market centres, now provide local services and Fivemiletown, across the county boundary in Tyrone, is an important service centre for the east of the area. Each of the villages has an individual character reflecting its historical development and situation.

Brookeborough, Maguiresbridge and Lisbellaw, by-passed by the main Belfast trunk road, are now quiet, residential centres. Brookeborough, named by its founders, the Brooke family, was once a busy administrative and market town, but today it is noted for its neat tree-lined Main Street. Maguiresbridge developed around the bridge marking the ancient crossing point of the Colebrooke River. Lisbellaw has its historic mill and Main Street but now sprawls informally across a hillside overlooked by the Church of Ireland. Tempo has a particularly attractive valley location adjoining the wooded demesne of Tempo Manor. Clabby, lacking the impressive 19th century street frontages of the other villages, is a loose cluster of buildings around a crossroads.

Conservation Interest and Issues

LANDSCAPE Broad lowland corridor with small rounded hills and long ridges: Well-farmed countryside with distinctive features associated with estates.

FARMING Intensive grassland production on generally progressive farms: Dairying, beef cattle and suckler herds.

WILDLIFE Hedges, woods, small loughs, rivers and bogs within farmed countryside.

WOODLAND AND FORESTRY Large, mature broad-leaf trees on estates, around farms and along roads: Estate woodland at Colebrooke and Tempo Manor: Small areas of private and State forestry.

HERITAGE Concentration of raths and tree-rings in the Colebrooke and Tempo valleys: Crannogs on Lough

Tempo Manor Gate Lodge

Eyes: Numerous Listed buildings associated with estates: Many traditional buildings and small country houses of character: Sites of corn and flax mills.

HOUSING AND DEVELOPMENT Older houses on the slopes and tops of drumlins: Traditional buildings still dominant: New bungalows adjacent to the main roads:

MINERAL WORKING Large limestone quarries at Crievehill: Sand and gravel extraction in Tempo River valley.

RECREATION AND TOURISM Roadside picnic spots: Limited provision for countryside recreation: Fishing on rivers and Lough Eyes: Local services in villages.

13 TOPPED AND BROUGHER MOUNTAIN UPLANDS

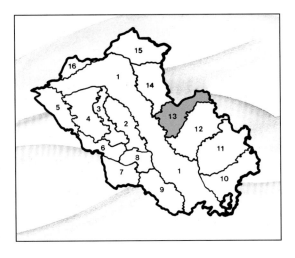

Landscape Character

To the east of Enniskillen between Tempo and Ballinamallard lies an upland area characterised by individual rounded hills - Topped Mountain, Ballyreagh, Derrin and Brougher Mountain. The eastern edge of the uplands is a prominent fault scarp bounded by the geological Tempo-Sixmilecross Fault. Along the fault, Old Red Sandstone containing hard conglomerates is uplifted, and these resistant rocks remain upstanding as hills, the different strata giving rise to a stepped profile on Brougher Mountain.

The rounded hills, which rise to over 660 feet (200 metres), are visible over a wide area of east Fermanagh. Their summits extend above a very broken upland plateau surface pitted with small loughs and dissected by steep glens, each choked with boulder clay forming drumlin hills.

Blanket peat covers the hilltops and there are extensive turf cuttings on Clabby Mountain. On the slopes there is a sharp contrast between the fields of improved grassland in the glens and the rough grassland, heath and bog of the hills. Recent reclamation has extended improved fields to the summits of the lower hills, for example at Ballyreagh. This mosaic of vegetation on the hills is attractive to curlew, lapwing and snipe and the loughs, with their surrounding willow scrub, provide an important wildlife habitat for warblers.

Field boundaries are varied, with locally occurring sandstone walls, earth banks with gorse or thorn and, in the valleys, low hedges with scattered trees. Woodland is to be found along the steeper valley sides, stream lines, around farms, or as willow scrub on bogs. Coniferous trees are notable features of planting around farms and in hedges. A number of small, scattered conifer plantations add to the already complex landscape variation.

Coolcran and Killyculla

Toppedmountain Lough

The upland area has a number of important archaeological sites. On the higher ground there are numerous prehistoric megalithic tombs, cairns and standing stones. The cairn on the summit of Topped Mountain is a distinctive landmark, visible over a wide area, but it represents only one of a whole complex of sites on and around the mountain. Monuments from the Early Christian period, principally raths, extend around the lower slopes of the hills. They are particularly aligned parallel to the Tempo Valley and concentrated at Cavanacarragh and Lisreagh on the western slopes of the hills.

The pattern of settlement today is largely derived from the distribution of farms in the 18th and 19th centuries. Small farms are dispersed along roads and lanes throughout the area with concentrations on south facing slopes. Some of the more isolated houses are now abandoned. Small estates with larger houses, like Ashfield House, are located on the lower slopes of Topped Mountain close to Enniskillen. A notable local characteristic is the use of unrendered dark red sandstone. New dwellings, often not associated with farms, have usually few of the traditional attributes of siting and design, and are located adjacent to roads.

There are no villages in the area but Ballyreagh, Mullanaskea, Garvary and Shankill are examples of small townland communities.

Conservation Interest and Issues

LANDSCAPE Upland area of individual rounded hills dissected by short, steep glens: Contrast between rough hill pasture or bog and improved agricultural fields.

FARMING Maintained small and medium-sized farms: Reclamation and intensive farming.

WILDLIFE Mixed land use on the hills, with bog, improved grassland and rough grazing: Small loughs: Important for breeding wader birds: Most of the bogs are disturbed by cutting.

WOODLAND AND FORESTRY Isolated patches and strips of coniferous trees on hill slopes: Mixed planting around farm buildings: Willow and birch scrub on cut-over bogs and around loughs.

HERITAGE Megalithic sites around Topped Mountain and on the slopes of Ballyreagh Hill and Brougher Mountain: Concentration of raths at lower altitudes: Good distribution of traditional buildings of varying scale.

HOUSING AND DEVELOPMENT Much older housing small and in poor condition: Local sandstone used in walls, houses and farm buildings: Replacement dwellings often have elevated roadside locations: Radio masts on Brougher Mountain.

MINERAL WORKING Some small sand and gravel pits.

RECREATION AND TOURISM Access to the summit cairn on Topped Mountain.

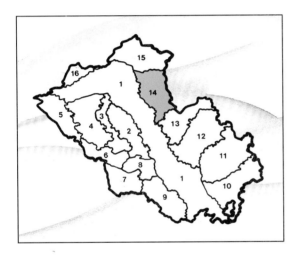

Landscape Character

Lying in north-east Fermanagh, surrounding the small towns of Ballinamallard and Irvinestown, is a broad area of lowland. The shores of Lower Lough Erne lie to the west and, to the east, the lowland stretches far into County Tyrone. Beyond its northern limit is the pronounced valley between Kesh and Lack.

The lowlands are underlain by beds of Old Red Sandstone which extend north from the Topped and Brougher Mountain Uplands to the Castle Archdale Fault, a major geological fault running from Lower Lough Erne north-east towards Omagh. North of the fault are youngerCarboniferous strata of shales, sandstones and limestones.

To the north of Irvinestown ice movement from east to west has tended to scour rather than deposit, thus exposing harder limestone crags lying in an east-west direction, eroding small lough basins, for example at Parkhill, and leaving a rocky hilly area between Aghagaffert, Tedd Cross Roads and Sheemuldoon.

South of Irvinestown, boulder clay has been deposited in lines of rounded drumlin hills, with a marked north-west to south-east trend. The linear hollows between the hills are generally low-lying, flat and often wide, but decreasing in width towards the higher land in the east.

Coolgarran

....The hills .... generally rise very abruptly from the bogs with which all the valleys abound, and as these hills are all cultivated to the top and divided into small fields and good quickset fences, and as almost every farmer's house has a small orchard attached to it, the country has the appearance of wealth....

O.S. Memoirs 1834 [13]

The Ballinamallard River is the only significant river in the area. Its main channel and numerous tributaries link the linear hollows in a complex drainage pattern. Although never dominant in the landscape, the valley with its often wooded slopes and boggy flood plains, is a local landscape feature.

In prehistoric times the damp valleys would have been difficult for travel and much of the land was probably forested, but farmers were attracted to the drier, lighter limestone soils of the north. Kiltierney with its Neolithic passage grave and Iron Age burials, has a long record of activity throughout prehistory, and elsewhere on the limestone there are megalithic tombs and standing stones.

In Early Christian times farming spread over much of

Kiltierney Deer Park

the area and raths were built on many prominent hills. In the same period, a crannog was built in Parkhill Lough and an abbey was founded within the deer park at Kiltierney.

The Ballinamallard-Irvinestown area is important for the agricultural industry in Fermanagh. Grass grows well on the more freely-draining hills and the land is managed intensively for silage and grazing. Cattle farming predominates and farm businesses are generally medium or large-sized. On the higher land in parts of the east and north of the area farms tend to be smaller, the land less free-draining, rush infestation more difficult to control and grazing the dominant use.

Throughout the area field boundaries are marked by hedges, often thick and uncut; broad-leaved trees in hedges and around houses give the countryside a very wooded appearance. In bogs and damp valley bottoms there are areas of birch, alder and willow scrub, for example at Drumbulcan and Derrycanny, and a sharp contrast between rough, wooded bogland and well-managed grassland is characteristic.

A different impression is given by the woodland and

Necarne

parkland of the Necarne estate. Mature broad-leaved woodlands almost surround Necarne castle and provide an enclosed scene on a grand scale, a magnificent setting for the castle.

The influence of the early 17th century Plantation settlement remains evident in the landscape today. In addition to the now derelict Necarne castle, large houses were built within smaller estates. Kiltierney deer park, part of the Castle Archdale estate, was enclosed with the thick stone wall which survives as a prominent feature. Many of the larger houses are of architectural interest

Ballinamallard

and most are in good repair. They are often imposing because of their hilltop locations, scale of farm buildings, walled yards and surrounding trees. However in some areas, especially near Tedd crossroads and Aghagaffert, north-east of Irvinestown, housing density is higher, buildings are smaller and there is some dereliction.

From the early 17th century Irvinestown and Ballinamallard developed as the two dominant commercial centres for the area. Irvinestown remains a busy service centre located adjacent to the Necarne estate. Its broad market place is overlooked by an 18th century church tower but some new buildings do not fit comfortably with the older 19th century architecture of the Main Street. Ballinamallard, now more residential, also retains an 18th century church tower among neat terraces of two-storey shops and houses.

LANDSCAPE Rolling drumlin lowlands with deep hollows and linear valleys: Good quality grassland with tall hedges, prominent hilltop farms and scattered woodlands: Broken rocky topography in north.

FARMING Intensive grassland production: Progressive farm businesses: Some smaller farms in north: Dairy and beef cattle.

WILDLIFE Scattered woodland, bogs, wet meadows, rivers and hedges.

WOODLAND AND FORESTRY Dense cover of trees in hedges and small woodlands: Mature woods and parkland on the Necarne estate: Birch and willow scrub on cut-over bogs.

HERITAGE Wide variety of sites: Kiltierney, site of prehistoric, Early Christian and Medieval activity: Necarne Castle and estate buildings.

HOUSING AND DEVELOPMENT Traditional siting and design in rural houses and farms: Ballinamallard and Irvinestown have attractive 19th century buildings: New development in and around the towns.

MINERAL WORKINGS Several small disused quarries on the limestone rocks in the north.

RECREATION AND TOURISM Limited facilities for countryside recreation: Proposed equestrian centre at Necarne estate: Fishing on the Ballinamallard River: Hotels and local services in Irvinestown and Ballinamallard.

15 GLENDARRAGH AND BANNAGH RIVER VALLEYS

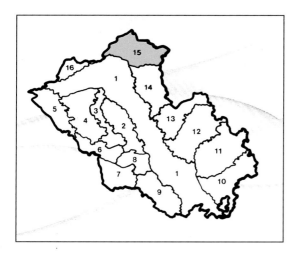

Landscape Character

The north-eastern tip of Fermanagh adjoining Counties Donegal and Tyrone is characterised by valley landscapes and steep drumlin hills. The land use is an alternating pattern of forest and farmland dissected by small rivers linking confined areas of bog and wet grassland between the drumlins. Uplands border the area to the east, their steep slopes divided by strips of fields and their rounded summits capped by blanket bog.

The underlying rocks are primarily Carboniferous shales, limestones and sandstones complicated by a south-west to north-east fault, the Cool Fault. In the east at Tappaghan Mountain and Largy much older, harder Dalradian schists are the foundations of the hills which extend eastwards into Tyrone.

The Cool Fault lies along the northern edge of the Glendarragh Valley, not a river valley in the true sense but really a broad glacial trough - an outlet for ice from its centre of accumulation in mid-Ulster. The ice sheets deposited small rounded hills on the floor of the Glendarragh valley but, further north, very large drumlin hills dominate the valley landscapes.

Land quality varies considerably within the area. The better-drained land on the hills in and around the Glendarragh valley is intensively farmed and grassland is managed for silage and grazing. Patterns of square fields are set in ladder strips on adjoining slopes such as Largy Hill. In the lowlands the hedges are often trimmed and the valley is notable for its tidy, well-managed appearance.

Glendarragh Valley

Edenaclogh and Bracklin

In the hilly drumlin area to the north around the Bannagh and Termon Rivers, soils are more difficult to drain and, although some small hay meadows survive, forestry has become increasingly important in the landscape. Major proportions of several large drumlins have been planted with coniferous trees and old estates at Clonelly and Tubbrid are also given over to forestry. Hedges and broad-leaf trees which have been retained within and around the plantations help to soften the landscape impact. On the upland fringe and in the flat hollows, peat soils are dominant and rough grassland and bog are characteristic. The mixture of wet grass-land, hay meadows and bogs provides habitats for curlew and snipe and small numbers of corncrakes still breed in the area.

From early times routeways from Donegal Bay and the Lough Erne basin to the Foyle Valley crossed this area. On the higher land and on rocky lowland, megalithic tombs, stone circles and standing stones are evidence of Neolithic and Bronze Age activity. At Drumskinny, in blanket bog beside the Kesh to Castlederg road, there is a well-preserved stone circle with a cairn and stone alignment. Ancient townland boundaries and their patterns reflect the surface topography, for example,

Formil townland is really one large drumlin. Raths appear on some hills in the Glendarragh and Termon valleys, but elsewhere their distribution is limited.

Settlement in the area is very much related to road patterns. Farmhouses are generally small, settlement density is low and the damper exposed high drumlins have not been favoured as housing sites. Farm buildings are traditional and dereliction is a feature of the more remote areas. Ederney and Lack are situated in the Glendarragh Valley astride the main route from Kesh to Omagh. Both are small tidy villages with well maintained 19th century street frontages and terraced housing. Pettigoe, in former days a local market centre related to several small estates, is now divided by the Border; lying half within Donegal and half within Fermanagh.

Kingfisher   *photo : Ron Thompson*

—80—

LANDSCAPE Contrasting area of valley, big drumlin and hillside landscapes: Large-scale patterns and contrasts of forest, farmland and lowland bog.

FARMING Local variation between intensively managed grassland, meadows and rush-infested pasture: Some farms being sold for forestry.

WILDLIFE Mosaic of hay meadow, bog, rough grazing and woodland of great value for wildlife: Important area for wader birds and corncrakes.

WOODLAND AND FORESTRY Forestry expanding on gley soils of drumlin hills: Incorporation of existing trees and hedges in plantations: Semi-natural woodland on cut-over bog and steep valley and drumlin sides.

HERITAGE Variety of archaeological sites represented including the stone circle at Drumskinny in State Care.

HOUSING AND DEVELOPMENT Sparsely popu-lated: Houses small and associated with farms: Road-side development in the Glendarragh valley: Estate buildings associated with Clonelly and Tubbrid: Small villages of Ederney and Lack retain character.

RECREATION AND TOURISM Few special facilities: Ulster Way crosses the area on county roads and forest tracks: Local services in Lack, Ederney and Pettigoe.

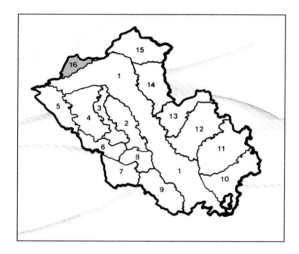

Landscape Character

In the north-west corner of Fermanagh, between Lower Lough Erne and the Border with Donegal, is a small triangle of countryside, about six miles across, which differs in character from any other part of Fermanagh. It lies on the southern edge of the Pettigoe plateau and despite its relatively low altitude, generally less than 500 feet (150 metres), it has a rough and rugged appearance. Rounded summits of Croagh and Mallybreen Hill rise above the plateau but are subdued by the conical peak of Breesy Hill, in Donegal.

The area is characterised by the underlying ancient metamorphic rocks - schists - harder and more acidic than the neighbouring Carboniferous limestones. Apart from the lower slopes and valleys, the plateau is glacially scoured, with numerous small loughs and rocky knolls. On the shallow slopes and in the depressions blanket bog has developed and now covers much of the landscape. The two principal rivers, the Garvary and Woodford rivers, have cut through small, rounded, glacial hills and terraces of sand and gravel on their route to Lower Lough Erne.

Lough Scolban and Keenaghan Lough lie on the

Keenaghan Lough

southern boundary of the area in a glacial trough parallel to the promontories and bays of Castle Caldwell. The loughs are underlain by the geological boundary between the schists to the north and the limestones to the south. The contrast of land use and landscape is remarkably abrupt, the north side of Keenaghan Lough being a rock-strewn open moorland of heath and bog, and the south side, enclosed, improved grasslands bounded by limestone walls and thorn hedges.

Farming has been concentrated on the boulder clay soils of the lower slopes and valleys. Here there is a dense pattern of hedged fields and clusters of small farms. Even on the higher plateau, low hills of boulder clay are picked out by old enclosures and trees planted around now-ruined farmsteads, for example at Tullyvogy and

Tullytrohan. Many of the farms continue to be worked at low intensity with a predominance of rough grazing and small hay meadows.

Beyond the enclosed fields is a broad, undulating expanse of moorland worked for turf. Old and new turf banks and areas cut by machine spread out from the roads and lanes. In the more remote areas, however, there are some of the most extensive areas of intact raised and blanket bog in Fermanagh. These moorlands support a significant population of moorland birds - golden plover, curlew, snipe, lapwing and dunlin. In the east of the area, conifer plantations cover a large part of Derrin Mountain, but some areas of blanket bog have been left unplanted to protect turbary rights.

Apart from crannogs in Derrintrig, Mallybreen and Rushen Loughs the area is distinguished by an absence of known archaeological sites. Undiscovered prehistoric sites may lie below the blanket bog.

Houses are loosely clustered in the valleys and around Lough Scolban. Small traditional farmhouses continue to be occupied, though often in a poor condition and with restricted services. Some houses are derelict and there is little evidence of replacement buildings. The eastern area around Derrin Mountain is largely depopulated and much land has been acquired for forestry. Brookhill House is situated at the eastern edge of the area, near Pettigoe across the Waterfoot River.

There are no villages within the area but there are small housing clusters in Derryrona and at the bridging point of the Garvary River.

Garvary River Valley

Conservation Interest and Issues

LANDSCAPE Edge of barren Pettigoe plateau broken by small river valleys: Open moorland, small loughs, forestry and traditional farming.

FARMING Marginal agricultural land: Traditional farm practices including haymaking and turbary: Rough grazing: Abandoned holdings and replacement by forestry.

WILDLIFE Extensive intact blanket bogs uncommon in Northern Ireland: Mixed moorland, bog and meadow provide important habitat for golden plover and other wader birds.

WOODLAND AND FORESTRY Scattered small trees and shrubs in hedges: Coniferous forestry on Derrin Mountain.

HERITAGE Some crannogs but otherwise few known archaeological sites.

HOUSING AND DEVELOPMENT Small traditional farmhouses many in poor condition.

MINERAL WORKING Small sand and gravel pits at Lough Scolban: Peat cutting on the blanket bog.

RECREATION AND TOURISM Recreation facilities limited and low key: Fishing at Lough Scolban and Keenaghan Lough: Ulster Way follows forest roads over Derrin Mountain: Isolated, despite proximity to Lough Erne.

FIGURE 1 LAND USE AND VEGETATION

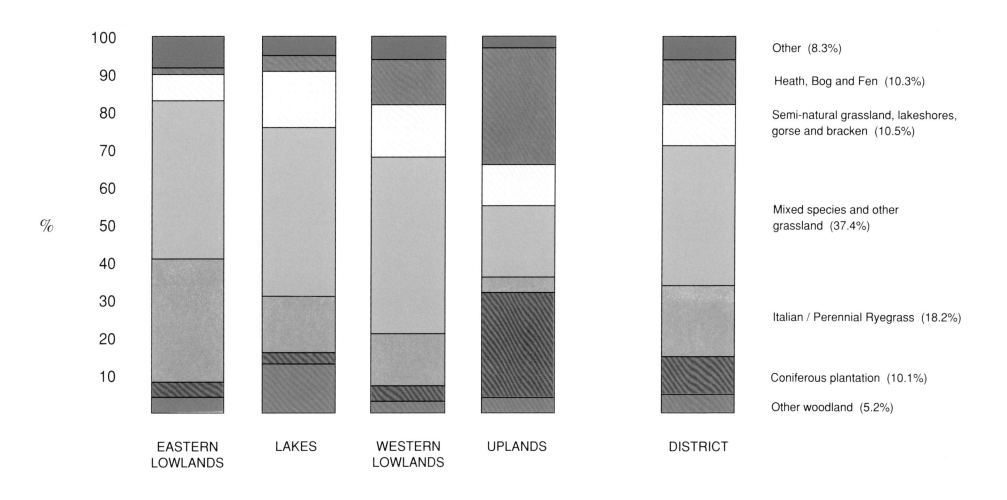

Other (8.3%)

Heath, Bog and Fen (10.3%)

Semi-natural grassland, lakeshores, gorse and bracken (10.5%)

Mixed species and other grassland (37.4%)

Italian / Perennial Ryegrass (18.2%)

Coniferous plantation (10.1%)

Other woodland (5.2%)

EASTERN LOWLANDS

LAKES

WESTERN LOWLANDS

UPLANDS

DISTRICT

%

Source : University of Ulster

FIGURE 2 NATURE CONSERVATION

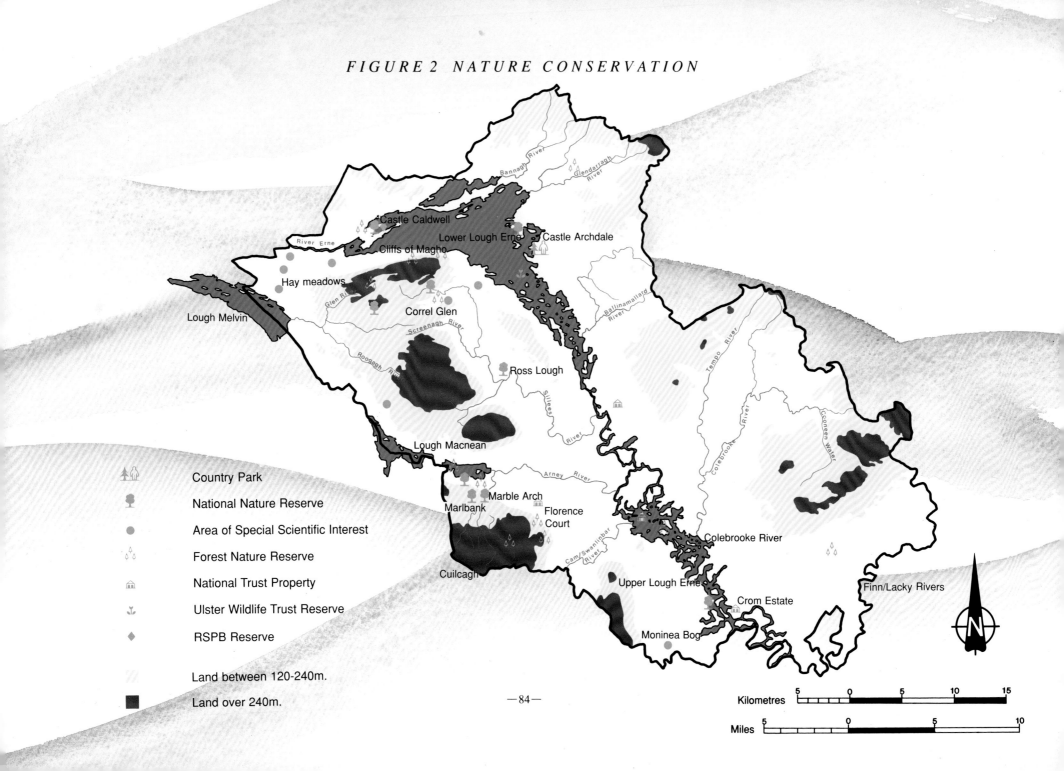

Castle Caldwell
Lower Lough Erne
Castle Archdale
Cliffs of Magho
Hay meadows
Correl Glen
Lough Melvin
Ross Lough
Lough Macnean
Marble Arch
Marlbank
Florence Court
Cuilcagh
Colebrooke River
Upper Lough Erne
Crom Estate
Finn/Lacky Rivers
Moninea Bog

River Erne
Bannagh River
Glendarragh River
Glen River
Screenagh River
Roogagh River
Ballinamallard River
Tempo River
Colebrooke River
Sillees River
Arney River
Cam/Swanlinbar River
Cooneen Water

Country Park

National Nature Reserve

Area of Special Scientific Interest

Forest Nature Reserve

National Trust Property

Ulster Wildlife Trust Reserve

RSPB Reserve

Land between 120-240m.

Land over 240m.

Kilometres 5 0 5 10 15

Miles 5 0 5 10

FIGURE 3 FORESTRY AND RECREATION

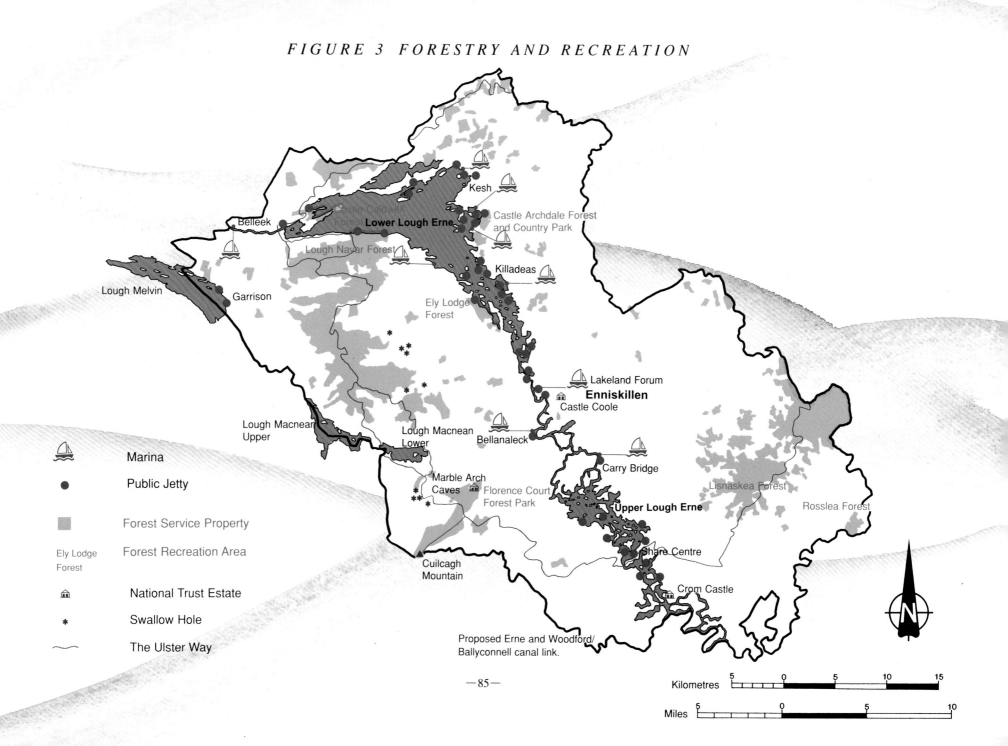

Kesh

Castle Caldwell Forest

Lower Lough Erne

Castle Archdale Forest and Country Park

Belleek

Lough Navar Forest

Killadeas

Lough Melvin

Garrison

Ely Lodge Forest

Lakeland Forum

Enniskillen

Castle Coole

Lough Macnean Upper

Lough Macnean Lower

Bellanaleck

Carry Bridge

Lisnaskea Forest

Marble Arch Caves

Florence Court Forest Park

Upper Lough Erne

Rosslea Forest

Share Centre

Cuilcagh Mountain

Crom Castle

⛵ Marina

● Public Jetty

▦ Forest Service Property

Ely Lodge Forest   Forest Recreation Area

⛩ National Trust Estate

✳ Swallow Hole

〜 The Ulster Way

Proposed Erne and Woodford/ Ballyconnell canal link.

Kilometres 5 0 5 10 15

Miles 5 0 5 10

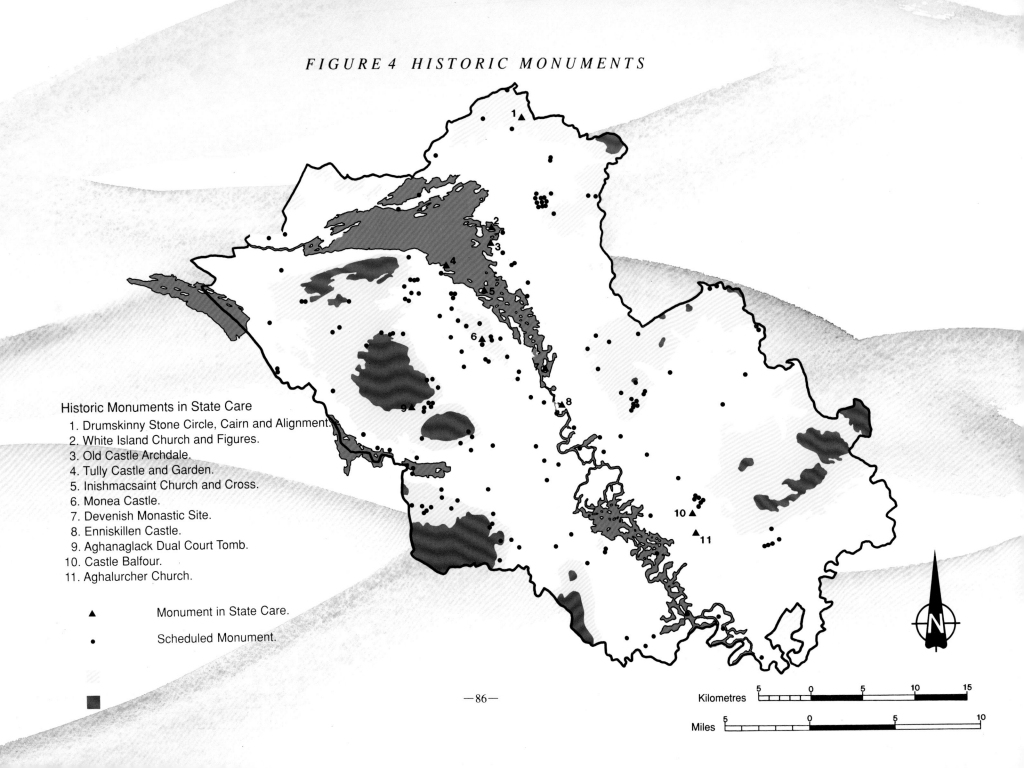

FIGURE 4 HISTORIC MONUMENTS

Historic Monuments in State Care

1. Drumskinny Stone Circle, Cairn and Alignment.
2. White Island Church and Figures.
3. Old Castle Archdale.
4. Tully Castle and Garden.
5. Inishmacsaint Church and Cross.
6. Monea Castle.
7. Devenish Monastic Site.
8. Enniskillen Castle.
9. Aghanaglack Dual Court Tomb.
10. Castle Balfour.
11. Aghalurcher Church.

▲   Monument in State Care.

•   Scheduled Monument.

Kilometres

Miles

FIGURE 5 NINETEENTH CENTURY LANDSCAPE

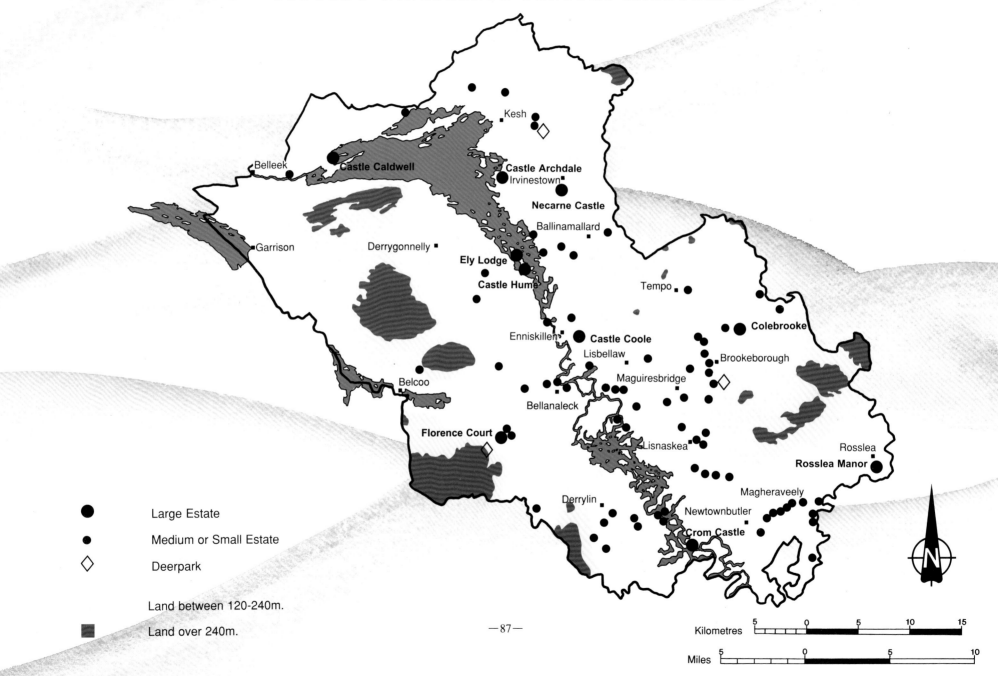

Belleek

Castle Caldwell

Kesh

Castle Archdale
Irvinestown

Necarne Castle

Garrison

Derrygonnelly

Ballinamallard

Ely Lodge

Castle Hume

Tempo

Enniskillen

Castle Coole

Colebrooke

Lisbellaw

Brookeborough

Belcoo

Maguiresbridge

Bellanaleck

Florence Court

Lisnaskea

Rosslea

Rosslea Manor

Derrylin

Magheraveely

Newtownbutler

Crom Castle

● Large Estate

• Medium or Small Estate

◇ Deerpark

Land between 120-240m.

Land over 240m.

Kilometres 5   0   5   10   15

Miles 5   0   5   10

N

APPENDIX 2

Glossary of Statutory Designations

DEPARTMENT OF THE ENVIRONMENT (NI)
ENVIRONMENTAL SERVICE
COUNTRYSIDE AND WILDLIFE BRANCH

1 Areas of Outstanding Natural Beauty (AONBs)
Areas of Outstanding Natural Beauty are areas of countryside with exceptional qualities of landscape, heritage and wildlife. An AONB is designated by the Department as part of the process of protecting and conserving these qualities and promoting their enjoyment. It is intended to be a positive contribution to rural development.

The purpose of designation is to provide a framework within which the Department may agree policies and proposals for :-
a. conserving or enhancing the natural beauty and amenities of the area;
b. conserving wildlife, historic features or natural phenomena within it;
c. promoting its enjoyment by the public; and
d. providing and maintaining public access to it.

These policies and proposals are drawn up in consultation with the people of the area, the District Council and all other interested parties.

Within the AONB, other public bodies in the exercise of their statutory responsibilities are obliged to give special consideration to the conservation of the countryside.

However, designation does not affect the ownership or occupation of the land and does not interfere with the duty and role of the District Council in the administration of the area.

AONBs are provided for by The Nature Conservation and Amenity Lands (NI) Order 1985.

2 Country Parks
Country Parks are areas of countryside, owned and managed by the Department for the purpose of promoting enjoyment and understanding of the countryside. Facilities include camping sites, nature trails, exhibitions and arrangements for a wide variety of activities.

Castle Archdale Country Park was established in 1974 under the Amenity Lands (NI) Act 1965. Visitors to the Park will find that the mixed woodlands, parklands and lake shore of the old estate are totally accessible. A marina, with full servicing for cruisers and other water-based sports and activities, lies in a sheltered bay just off the Lower Lough. Since the Park is not adjacent to local towns, the extensive caravan and camping site is particularly useful for overnight stays or holidays. Part of the 18th century manor house courtyard has been refurbished to house the Park Centre, while another portion is a modern Youth Hostel.

3 National Nature Reserves (NNRs)
National Nature Reserves are nationally important sites representing the best examples of wildlife habitats existing in Northern Ireland. They are managed specifically to conserve nature and for education or research. While most have open access some are restricted due to the need for protection. Nearly all are in public ownership by the Department of the Environment or the Department of Agriculture, Forest Service.

Until the introduction of The Nature Conservation and Amenity Lands (NI) Order 1985 the appropriate legislation was the Amenity Lands Act (NI) 1965.

4 Other Nature Reserves
In addition to NNRs there are other sites of regional importance for nature conservation which may be especially suitable for education, research or public enjoyment. These Nature Reserves may be owned or leased and managed by the Department of the Environment, the Department of Agriculture Forest Service, the District Councils and voluntary bodies, such as the Ulster Wildlife Trust, the Royal Society for Protection of Birds and the National Trust. The Reserves are generally managed by agreement with the Department.

5 Areas of Special Scientific Interest (ASSIs)
Areas of Special Scientific Interest are recognised as regionally, nationally or internationally important sites for nature conservation. They include the best examples

of a range of habitats such as bogs, woodland and meadows, as well as sites of interest for their geology or for rare species. ASSIs need not be publicly owned but they are protected against damaging land use or management changes. Management agreements allow for voluntary co-operation between landowners and the Department and, where necessary, compensating payments may be agreed. There is no right of access to sites in private ownership.

ASSIs are identified and declared under the provisions of The Nature Conservation and Amenity Lands (NI) Order 1985. The programme of surveying and declaration of sites will continue over a number of years.

6 Areas of Scientific Interest (ASIs)

Areas of Scientific Interest were designated under the Amenity Lands Act (NI) 1965 because of their flora, fauna, geological or physiographical features. They are protected from development because of their scientific interest but they are now being replaced to some extent with ASSIs.

HISTORIC MONUMENTS AND BUILDINGS BRANCH

7 State Care Monuments

State Care sites are historic monuments which are owned or held in guardianship and maintained by the Department. The sites represent some of the most important and best preserved monuments in Northern Ireland. They are generally open to the public. Explanatory notices and facilities for visitors are often provided.

Acquisition and management of State Care sites is provided for by the Historic Monuments Act (NI) 1971.

8 Scheduled Monuments

Scheduled monuments are other important historic monuments and sites which although in private owner-ship are Scheduled for protection under the Historic Monuments Act (NI) 1971. There is no right of access to most of these monuments and visitors are advised to seek the landowner's permission. Advice on all historic monuments and archaeological finds is provided by the Department. Most archaeological sites are not Scheduled but this does not minimise their importance.

9 Listed Buildings

Listed buildings are buildings of special architectural or historic interest. Buildings are selected for Listing by the Department with the advice of the Historic Buildings Council and the relevant District Council. Only a few listed buildings are open to the public on a regular basis. The Planning (NI) Order 1972 and The Planning and Building Regulations (Amendment) (NI) Order 1990 set out the legal requirements relating to Listing. All proposals for alteration or demolition, both partial and complete, must be first approved by the Department.

TOWN AND COUNTRY PLANNING SERVICE

10 Conservation Areas

Conservation Areas are built-up areas of special architectural or historic interest, the character and appearance of which it is desirable to preserve and enhance. They are designated under the provisions of The Planning (NI) Order 1972. The Enniskillen Conservation Area was designated in 1987. It is the only such Area in Fermanagh District.

DEPARTMENT OF AGRICULTURE (NI)

11 Environmentally Sensitive Areas (ESAs)

Environmentally Sensitive Area schemes are designed to help conserve those areas of high landscape and/or wildlife value which are vulnerable to changes in farming practices. Under the voluntary schemes payments are offered to farmers willing to maintain or convert to environmentally beneficial farming practices.

ESAs are designated under the provisions of The Agriculture (Environmental Areas) (NI) Order 1987.

APPENDIX 3 : USEFUL ADDRESSES

Countryside & Wildlife Branch
Department of the Environment (NI)
Calvert House
23 Castle Place
Belfast BT1 1FY
Tel: 0232 230560

Country Park & Nature Reserves Wardens
Countryside & Wildlife Branch
Department of the Environment (NI)
Castle Archdale Country Park
Irvinestown, Co Fermanagh
Tel: 03656 21588

Historic Monuments & Buildings Branch
Department of the Environment (NI)
5-33 Hill Street
Belfast BT1 2LR
Tel: 0232 235000

Environmental Protection Division
Department of the Environment (NI)
Calvert House
23 Castle Place
Belfast BT1 1FY
Tel: 0232 230560

Town & Country Planning Service
Department of the Environment for (NI)
County Buildings
East Bridge Street
Enniskillen, Co Fermanagh
Tel: 0365 327270

County Executive Office & Forest Service
Department of Agriculture (NI)
Inishkeen House
Killyhevlin Industrial Estate
Enniskillen, Co Fermanagh
Tel: 0365 325004

Lough Erne Warden
Department of Agriculture (NI)
Wardens Office
Castle Lane
Portora
Enniskillen, Co Fermanagh
Tel: 0365 322836

Drainage Division
Department of Agriculture for (NI)
Riversdale
Ballinamallard, Co Fermanagh
Tel: 036581 520 or 529

Fermanagh District Council
Town Hall
Enniskillen Co Fermanagh
Tel: 0365 325050

Tourist Information Department
Fermanagh District Council
Lakeland Visitor Centre
Shore Road
Enniskillen, Co Fermanagh
Tel: 0365 323110

County Museum
Fermanagh District Council
Enniskillen, Co Fermanagh
Tel: 0365 325050

Northern Ireland Tourist Board
River House
48 High Street
Belfast BT1 2DS
Tel: 0232 231221 (Admin)
     0232 246609 (Tourist Information)

Royal Society for the Protection of Birds
Local Warden
Castlecaldwell
Belleek, Co Fermanagh
Tel: 036565 328

Conservation Volunteers
Local Office
Castle Archdale Country Park
Irvinestown, Co Fermanagh
Tel: 03656 28184

National Trust
Rowallane House
Saintfield
Ballynahinch BT24 7LH
Tel: 0238 510721

Ulster Wildlife Trust
Barnett's Cottage
Barnett Demesne
Malone Road
Belfast BT9 5PB
Tel: 0232 612236

APPENDIX 4 : FOOTNOTES

1   Dean William Henry's Account of County
Fermanagh c. 1739, p4; The Public Library, Armagh.

2   Ordnance Survey Memoirs of Ireland (1834-5),
Parishes of Fermanagh, Vol. 4, Parish of Aghalurcher,
p9; The Institute of Irish Studies, The Queen's
University of Belfast and The Royal Irish Academy,
Dublin; 1990.

3   Dean William Henry's Account of County
Fermanagh c.1739, p4; The Public Library, Armagh.

4   Cruickshank and McHugh, County Fermanagh; in
Leslie Symons (Ed.), Land Use in Northern Ireland,
p242; University of London Press Ltd; 1963.

5   Robert Harbinson, Song of Erne, p45;
The Blackstaff Press, Dundonald.

6   Robert Harbinson, Song of Erne, p45;
The Blackstaff Press, Dundonald.

7   William Parke, A Fermanagh Childhood, p1;
The Friar's Bush Press, Belfast; 1988.

8   Ordnance Survey Memoir Transcriptions (1834),
Parish of Inishmacsaint, p2; The Institute of Irish
Studies, The Queen's University of Belfast and The
Royal Irish Academy, Dublin.

9   Gareth Jones, Hidden Landscapes; in The Book of
the Irish Countryside, p67; The Blackstaff Press,
Dundonald; 1987.

10   Henry Glassie, Irish Folk History, p9;
The O'Brien Press Ltd, Dublin; 1982.

11   Peter Flanagan, Saint Naile; in Henry Glassie,
Irish Folk History, p23; The O'Brien Press Ltd,
Dublin; 1982.

12   Ordnance Survey Memoirs of Ireland (1834-5),
Parishes of Fermanagh, Vol.4, Parish of Kinawley,
p123; The Institute of Irish Studies, The Queen's
University of Belfast and The Royal Irish Academy,
Dublin; 1990.

13   Ordnance Survey Memoir Transcriptions (1834),
Parish of Magheracross, p11; The Institute of
Irish Studies, The Queen's University of Belfast and The
Royal Irish Academy, Dublin.

Printed in the United Kingdom for HMSO
Dd. 8245945, C35, 3/91